CRISIS PROOF LEADERSHIP

CRISIS PROOF LEADERSHIP

WHERE OPPORTUNITY MEETS PREPARATION

BETH RASHLEIGH

NEW DEGREE PRESS

COPYRIGHT © 2021 BETH RASHLEIGH

CRISIS PROOF LEADERSHIP

Where Opportunity Meets Preparation

ISBN   978-1-63730-663-5   *Paperback*
        978-1-63730-752-6   *Kindle Ebook*
        978-1-63730-938-4   *Ebook*

For Sam. I hope this book makes the world a little bit more worthy of the amazing person you already are.

TABLE OF CONTENTS

INTRODUCTION

If you had to choose between docking a cruise ship full of people infected with a highly contagious virus or sending them away to try and find another place to dock, what would you choose?

In the early months of 2020, the COVID-19 virus began infecting the world. In the midst of this, a unique challenge was brewing at sea. Cruise ships, known for being super-spreaders of disease under normal circumstances due to their tight quarters, were starting to fill with COVID-19 positive passengers. Passengers and crew members were from all over the world. Which country should take the passengers, who were now patients? They were turned away at port after port. No one wanted them. Fear around the spread of the virus was real, and concerns about both the potential consequences to residents where the ships might dock and their hospital systems were leading to a lack of ownership of the problem. The ships quickly became floating hospitals that were ill-equipped to provide care to COVID-19 passengers.

Several of these ships were just off the coast of Florida. As they started to run out of supplies and the sick became sicker, they sent a mayday message to shore for help. That's where Monica Cepero entered the story. Monica is the County Administrator for Broward County Florida. She leads and manages over 6,500 county employees who do everything from providing human services to the county's population of over two million to airport management. That oversight also includes the management and operation of Port Everglades, where the ships were hoping to dock and get the help they desperately needed. The county had a decision to make. When we spoke, Monica said,

> "It was so early on in the pandemic and one of the primary concerns was that the passengers would get off the ship and could potentially spread this virus throughout the community. But the ships were running out of oxygen, medication, and other supplies needed to adequately care for the sick. They needed to come to shore as soon as possible. Every other port had denied their request to take these passengers. There were not only US citizens on board these ships, but there were many others from all around the world as well. The individuals on these ships could be our neighbors, parents, friends, or loved ones. The only thing I could focus on was the humanity of it. It became a humanitarian issue that was urgently in need of a solution. These people were in the middle of a crisis, and we were in a position to help. We have to remember as leaders that everyone looks to us, and we have to be honest and empathetic in tough situations and never lose sight of things at the human level."

Broward County, which oversees the port, allowed the ships to dock, airlifted critical patients to local hospitals, and worked with the many layers and complexities of government and various jurisdictions to ensure that the passengers got the care they needed and that the others were provided safe passage home. Why? It was the right thing to do.

This story, and many others like it, got me thinking about leadership during times of crisis. So many people were struggling during the pandemic. But I noticed that individuals like Monica were able to continue to lead, and some have even thrived during crisis after crisis that seemed to appear throughout the year. I wondered if she was unique or part of a larger trend, and what I have found has transformed the way I think about crisis leadership.

Before the pandemic hit, the world was already experiencing another crisis: burnout. Job burnout has been recognized as an "occupational phenomenon." In fact, the World Health Organization added burnout to the ICD-11, and it's now an official medical diagnosis.

A new survey reported in Tech Republic conducted in July 2020 found that "75 percent of workers have experienced burnout, and 40 percent of those polled said it was a direct result of the coronavirus pandemic."

Leaders are now dealing with a trifecta of leadership challenges—a burned-out workforce, many of who they are now leading remotely, and a growing mental health crisis.

It would be easy to think that the strongest, toughest, most cutthroat leaders would be the ones that would thrive in this environment, but my research found just the opposite. Highly empathetic, focused, values-driven leaders have been better able to keep their teams engaged and thriving.

Crisis isn't a great time to find out who you are as a leader. In order to thrive, you need to know who you are before a crisis hits. The stronger your foundation is, the more it holds when a crisis occurs.

Exceptional crisis leadership happens when opportunity meets preparation.

I have a deep belief that we are all put on earth for a purpose. Mine is to help people become the leaders the world needs them to be. I found my passion when I was twenty-two, working my first job out of college. I was hired to be a recruiter at a small Indianapolis-area county hospital. Because I wasn't coming in with a strong healthcare or nursing background, I had to get to work building relationships.

I shadowed department and nursing leaders, as well as the staff holding positions I would be filling. I asked questions like, *"What makes someone a good fit for an Intensive Care Unit (ICU) nurse vs. an Emergency Department (ED) nurse?" and "What the heck does a Respiratory Therapist do?"* I approached learning the organization like a class. Within about a year, I was gaining credibility as someone who understood what it took to hire the right person for the job.

Unfortunately, that's when I discovered another problem: turnover. Turnover in healthcare is always on the higher end. The jobs are in high demand and candidates often receive multiple offers and large sign-on bonuses. In the last twenty-five years, that hasn't changed. When I started analyzing trends, we had turnover in the areas where leaders were struggling to lead. If I was going to get these candidates to stay, I'd have to find a way to tackle that issue.

With the truly blind optimism only a twenty-three-year-old can have, I pitched the idea of a leadership newsletter to my boss and then started researching what the best leaders do each and every day. Little did I know, my true calling was becoming clearer in that moment.

Upon finishing my master's degree, I was given the opportunity to work for the Central Intelligence Agency. After working in various training roles for a few years, I started to facilitate leadership development classes full time. That was over ten years ago, and I've never looked back. I love standing in the front of a classroom answering questions about how we can best serve the people we lead. I love opening someone up to a new way of thinking or a new tool that can help them carry the sometimes-heavy burden of leadership. I love supporting and affirming leaders on the phone as I coach them through tough conversations or challenges. Leadership is my love language.

In 2019, I left the corporate space and started my own coaching and consulting business. I have the privilege of working with leaders to help them solve day-to-day challenges through team development and one-on-one coaching. As

I've worked with my clients through these big recent events, I have had a front row seat to the impact burnout and crisis leadership are having. I see more crispy burnt humans in my practice than ever, and as I work to help those leaders get to the other side of this crisis, I want to share what I'm learning and what's working for my clients.

This book is for people who are currently leading a team and those who one day want to step into a leadership role. My hope is that as you read it, you feel like you have someone in your corner helping you build new skills and refine habits while arming you with tools that will help you lead your team. As we dive deep into relevant topics, you'll hear stories from other leaders about what's working and what's not, and you will have the opportunity to complete activities that will help you apply what you are learning.

Your journey to becoming a crisis proof leader starts now.

PART 1

HOW WE GOT HERE

CHAPTER ONE

CRISIS AND LEADERSHIP

"Anyone can lead when the plan is working. The best lead when the plan falls apart."

—ROBIN SHARMA

I've spent most of my career working in organizations where the mission is related to keeping people alive. Crisis is part of the organizational DNA of healthcare. Perhaps the most notable example of this is from recent history. In 2020, when the first case of COVID-19 in Indiana came through the emergency room, hospital leaders realized that a coordinated response plan was needed, and quickly.

Shannon Kunberger, the former Executive Director of Network Nursing for Community Health Network, a large Indianapolis area healthcare network, noticed right away that many other leaders were struggling to make decisions as the crisis became apparent. But because Shannon has worked in high pressure, high stress environments her whole career, including many years as a flight nurse, she has trained her body to react differently. She told me, "My brain just started going right into that rapid fire of how do I operationalize this one breath at a time, one step at a time." She used that ability to help quickly set up a command center for the organization to ensure that patients and staff knew what to do with suspected cases of COVID-19.

Leaders like Shannon find a way to function through the crisis and still get results for their organization and teams.

We throw the word crisis around often, but let's really dissect what it means for the purpose of this book and for leadership in general. The official definition has three possibilities according to Oxford Languages Online. The first is "a time of intense difficulty, trouble or danger." Sounds about right to me. The second definition adds in "a time when a difficult or important decision must be made." Finally, a crisis can also be "the turning point of a disease when an important change takes place, indicating either recovery or death."

To simplify, a crisis is a time of difficulty where we need to continue to make difficult and important decisions that can lead to either recovery or destruction. Examples could include everything from getting sick or injured, being harassed at work, getting a divorce, job loss, a company buyout, or a global pandemic.

A workplace crisis that needs to be managed by leaders will typically contain three additional elements.

1. **A threat to the organization.**
2. **The element of surprise.**
3. **A short decision time. (Management Study HQ, 2021)**

Based on this definition, how often do you think crisis is happening in the workplace? Monthly, weekly, daily? I think for many leaders, a crisis is happening every single day. That's why we have to shift the way we think about crisis leadership. It's not a rare occurrence. We need to be prepared to lead this way often.

It might seem like there is only bad news here, but Leadership Coach and Consultant Mark Ferrara, who has spent his career working with leaders at Fortune 500 companies like Eli Lilly and Disney, has a saying that one should "never waste a good crisis." He noticed that "interestingly enough, crisis in and of itself is a great teacher. Crisis naturally creates opportunities for vision, alignment, motivation and inspiration. People are also more naturally intrinsically motivated because the goal is clear. If you can capitalize on those things, they will make a difference during times of crisis."

However, to do that you'll need to be able to overcome some biological factors. Crisis often creates higher than usual amounts of stress, and research shows that stress impairs our core cognitive functions. Surprisingly, this is fairly new research. For years we believed that stress sharpened our brains. Researchers have recently established that "stress makes decision making (at the individual as well as collective levels) more irrational, hurried, and unsystematic. Furthermore, stress can impair working memory, increase distraction, lower reaction time, and reduce our very ability to process information. That's not even the half of it. Decision making under stress makes us a lot more susceptible to group pressures, prejudices, and constraints. The exact antithesis of effective crisis decision making." (Noggin Online)

To fully understand the potential impacts at work, it's important to understand what happens to our brains during stress. It's been proven that our cerebral cortex and the limbic system kick in when we are making decisions under stress. The cerebral cortex helps with problem solving while the limbic system scans for danger. (Noggin Online)

Because stress triggers our survival instincts, the limbic system overrides our cerebral cortex. Researchers know that "when it does that, we lose our inductive, deductive, abstract, and even logical thinking faculties—all of which are of supreme importance when we need to effectively deal with crisis. (Noggin Online)

All this biology encourages us to quickly navigate and resolve crisis situations to get our body and brain back to a normal state. In a crisis, your brain is going to want to make decisions or avoid the situation altogether, but those decisions will not always be the best ones because the problem-solving part of your brain may not be at the table.

Heather Haas, President of ADVISA and Leadership Development Expert has noticed that leadership crisis response tends to fall into one of three buckets. The first is a head in the sand leader. She says, "Some people are just slow to acknowledge and name what's going on and instead of putting plans in place they deny that something is happening and hope it goes away."

Then there are the people on the other side of the spectrum who she calls the knee jerk leaders. She says, "These leaders tend to favor high levels of control and big, sweeping, swift decisions that don't take into account anyone's emotional state. Finally, there are leaders who walk in the middle and lead with data, facts and empathy."

These leaders are getting the best results and become truly crisis proof leaders.

I've seen the knee jerk reaction leaders in crisis many times in my career firsthand. My very first assignment at the CIA was to provide training and project management support for an IT system. Unfortunately, the project was plagued by technical challenges and a lack of support from key stakeholders. Nine months into my career at the CIA, the project was shut down.

I still remember finding out about the project closure. They pulled all the staff into a conference room and told us that we would still have jobs with the CIA, but that we needed to find new roles. We had sixty days to find roles ourselves, or we would be "placed," likely in jobs we wouldn't be thrilled about. The project's contractors, mostly software engineers, would be reassigned or fired by their parent organizations as soon as the project was fully shut down.

As the shutdown process began, I struggled. I was shell shocked by the quick decision to shut down and mourning the loss of my work family. Like so many leaders in times of crisis, the leadership team jumped right into action. Within hours of the shutdown meeting, they had found places for several staff and contractors on another project team. Some of the team would be able to stay together in this new group.

On the surface that felt amazing. I still had a job. I could continue to work with people that I knew and respected. But the reality of that transition was far from amazing. As the teams merged, tensions were high. The role I served on our existing team was already being done by someone else. I wanted to know what my role was going to be, and my counterpart wanted reassurance that she wasn't being pushed out. To say that relationship started out on rocky footing would be a massive understatement. I wasn't the only one experiencing this pushback. Many of my coworkers were in similar situations.

When I look back now, I can see how in the rush to solve a crisis issue and take care of the team, decisions were made quickly and without understanding the very real impact they could have on the people involved. That new team experienced an increase in turnover as I and others like me decided the roles weren't in our best interest and we moved onto other projects. Too often in times of crisis, leaders look for a short-term solution without thinking about the long-term implications or they make decisions from a place of fear.

I've also seen head in the sand leaders in action and have been one myself from time to time. One of the most common crisis situations that leaders want to hide from is employee performance issues. You start to notice that things are getting missed or work isn't being completed according to procedure, and instead of providing feedback or training, you hope it will get better on its own. Spoiler alert, it doesn't. Instead, the problem compounds. Discussing performance problems kindly and as quickly as possible is a much more effective approach when we can force ourselves to take it.

Conversely, crisis proof leaders walk that middle road and keep their teams walking with them. A great example of that approach is the way the Tylenol tampering scandal was handled by leaders at Johnson & Johnson in 1982. Back in the days before tamper proof packaging, an individual took packages of Tylenol capsules off the shelves at a store and added cyanide to them, resulting in the deaths of three individuals.

Immediately the company expressed horror that deaths were occurring and offered a $100,000 reward for the killer. It then stopped all manufacturing of Tylenol capsules and recalled all of the product from shelves, removing over twenty-two million bottles of medicine. All of the recalled product was voluntarily destroyed to ensure no one else would be injured or killed. (Knight, 1982)

This crisis should have spelled the end of Tylenol, and many at the time didn't think that the product would ever be sold on shelves again. If they had just buried their heads in the sand and waited for the authorities to resolve the issue, it likely would have spelled the end of the Tylenol brand. It would have been equally disastrous to jump in and blame the murderer instead of trying to address customers' very real fears. But the swift handling of this tragic incident, which did not happen as a result of any company fault, is a textbook example of crisis proof leadership and allowed them to win back customer confidence and loyalty.

This happened in part because Johnson and Johnson's values were clear and part of how the company had always done business. Through the crisis, they repeatedly went back to their values, which as stated on their website include: "We believe our first responsibility is to the patients, doctors and nurses, to mothers and fathers and all others who use our products and services. We are responsible to the communities in which we live and work and to the world community as well." Johnson & Johnson's values drove their decision-making response, even when they were advised by others to protect themselves from lawsuits.

Crises, big and small, are going to happen on your leadership journey. It's not a question of if, but when. The more prepared you are as a leader, the better equipped you will be to survive and thrive.

Reflection Activity: Think of a crisis moment in your leadership journey. Which leadership style did you most closely use? What was the impact of that style? What's one adjustment you could make the next time you face a crisis to be a crisis proof leader?

CRISIS AND LEADERSHIP RECAP:

- A crisis is a time of difficulty where we need to continue to make difficult and important decisions that can lead to either recovery or destruction.
- Our brains can work against us in times of stress and lead us to make faster, more terrible decisions.
- Leaders often fall into the trap of making knee jerk reactions or burying their heads in the sand. Neither is an effective leadership technique.
- The more prepared we are ahead of the crisis, the better our odds for success and survival.

CHAPTER 2

WHY NOW?

———

"Let us all be the leaders we wish we had."

—SIMON SINEK

Imagine you are standing on a platform in the middle of a lake. Suddenly it bursts into flames. You don't know how to swim and have never wanted to learn, but a swim coach appears and offers a lesson. Do you allow yourself to be coached out of the crisis? Of course you do, because you have a need to learn it.

Sometimes we need a push to get us to do things that we've always known are a good idea in theory. We need that burning platform to give us the motivation to learn something new or take a risk. If you've been putting off your own development as a leader, now is the time to take the leap. Leading through crisis is becoming the norm, not the exception. Increasingly burned-out employees, a mental health crisis, and remote work just added fuel to an already burning platform.

 ***Reflection Activity:*** *What is your burning platform? What has been standing in the way of your development? Why do you want to develop yourself as a leader right now? What will push you to set aside the time you will need?*

BURNOUT

The World Health Organization has officially classified burnout as an occupational phenomenon. They define burnout as a formula: burnout equals emotional exhaustion plus disillusionment plus withdrawal. They further clarify that "burnout is a syndrome conceptualized as resulting from chronic workplace stress that has not been successfully managed." It is characterized by three factors:

- feeling depleted or exhausted
- feeling negativity or cynicism about work
- reduced professional effectiveness.

According to a Gallup study conducted in 2020, 76 percent of employees experience burnout symptoms at least sometimes. We can only assume that number is now higher. The causes vary, but research from Healthline shows that "being exposed to continual stress can cause us to burnout. Feelings of exhaustion, anxiety, and isolating from friends and family members can be some of the signs."

Recent events have pushed some companies to jump into action. At LinkedIn, employees were given an extra paid week off. The entire company is getting the time off as an opportunity to unplug, recharge, and avoid burnout. "We wanted to make sure we could give them something really valuable, and what we think is most valuable right now is time for all of us to collectively walk away," said Teuila Hanson, LinkedIn's chief people officer, who joined the company in June 2020 to CNN. "Since everyone is off at the same time, that means workers aren't inundated by emails, meeting notes and project requests piling up in their absence."

Stress is a contributing factor to burnout, but it's certainly not the only cause. When I moved back to the Indianapolis area, I started working at a biomedical equipment repair company. My job was to design and facilitate leadership development programs for the company, and I loved it. Despite exponential growth, the company had managed to keep its start-up culture and family feel. That all shifted when about two years into the position, when the division I worked for was sold. Luckily, I kept my job. But the two years that followed were hard. The culture of the company changed quickly as a new executive leadership team was hired. Processes and procedures were changed. Departments were restructured. I quickly became less of a leadership coach and more of a mental health counselor as employees struggled with the changes. Add that to shifting priorities in my own role along with direction changes I wasn't sure I could support, and I got burned out really quickly.

Unfortunately, it took me almost two full years to leave the company and address my burnout symptoms. Why? I liked the people. I had no trouble leaving the organization as a whole, but leaving the humans was a whole other story. Eventually, I could no longer ignore my own body. I was exhausted both physically and mentally. I needed a change and luckily found a position that was both a step up and the culture reset I badly needed. The true cause of burnout for me in this situation was a lack of connection to the company.

As I've coached and worked with leaders over the years, time management also often appears as a cause of burnout. People feel like they just can't keep up with the pace at work, which leads to life feeling unbalanced at home. Stay in that state too long and it's difficult to avoid the symptoms of burnout even if you really love the work you are doing.

MENTAL HEALTH CRISIS

Amen Research Clinic reports that a 2020 Census Bureau poll shows that one-third of Americans have signs of anxiety or depression, or both. This is a huge increase compared to pre-pandemic numbers. In an average year, an estimated 18 percent of Americans are affected by anxiety disorders but 30 percent are currently experiencing symptoms. The news on depression is even worse. The number of people reporting depressive symptoms during the pandemic is twice as high as 2014 data. But depression and anxiety aren't the only mental health issues present in the work environment.

Adam Grant wrote an amazing article about an underappreciated mental health condition called languishing. He says, "Languishing is a sense of stagnation and emptiness. It feels as if you're muddling through your days, looking at your life through a foggy windshield. Languishing dulls your motivation, disrupts your ability to focus, and triples the odds that you'll cut back on work. People who are languishing struggle with internal motivation and concentration, which could be catastrophic for employees in critical roles like medicine where lives are on the line."

When this article came out, it was shared widely. I saw at least twenty-five social media posts about it on the day it came out. It hit a nerve with people. I think it gave language to how so many people were feeling. The takeaway for leaders here is that languishing "appears to be more common than major depression—and in some ways it may be a bigger risk factor for mental illness." Research suggests that "the people most likely to experience major depression and anxiety disorders in the next decade aren't the ones with those symptoms today. They're the people who are languishing right now." (Grant, 2021)

If you have employees identifying as languishing, they are much more likely to struggle down the road. Leaders play a critical role in helping identify employees who may be struggling, supporting them as they navigate their symptoms and providing help and resources for their long-term mental health.

LEADING REMOTELY

As offices shut down around the world and social distancing became mandated, many leaders were suddenly leading a team of remote workers. Although there can certainly be positives about working from home, like the ability to throw in a load of laundry or cuddle your pet throughout the day, it also presents real problems. Organizational cultures often are built and reinforced in the day-to-day interactions around the office. Without them, how do companies ensure that culture survives?

Additionally, research is identifying a ton of challenges with remote work. ZDNet reports that one study shows that "over one-third of office workers say that 'email fatigue is likely to push them to quit their jobs.' One in three (33 percent) of employees say an excess of video calls is the most unpleasant part of remote work. Over two in five (44 percent) of remote workers dream of the day without video calls and one in four (25 percent) crave a notification-free day." That's a large chunk of workers who are struggling to keep up with remote work and all that comes with it.

"The data is clear: the massive shift to remote work and digital communications is making employees fatigued and burned out," said Rahul Vohra, founder and CEO of Superhuman. "Companies must urgently adopt tools and policies that will make employees happy and productive, regardless of where they work." (Brown, 2021)

But it's not all bad news. Many employees and organizations are seeing the benefits of remote work. Another study from Gartner "finds that about 70 percent of employees wish to continue some form of remote work. Twitter and Facebook have already given their employees permission to work remotely on a permanent basis." (George, 2021)

Leaders who have been suddenly thrust into leading remotely see the pros and cons. I interviewed Karly Cope, vice president of Talent for Community Health Network. She says one of the positives of remote work is that "from a talent perspective, that allows me to recruit from a whole new pool of people, so I've now got remote positions that used to be on site. I can hire anyone from anywhere to sit anywhere." The cons are there too. She also says working remotely can be "incredibly isolating. We talk on the phone on the computer in calls all day long, but you're still isolated. You're here in your four walls, all day, every day. It's so monotonous."

Although the jury still seems to be out on working remotely, what is very clear is that leaders are struggling to lead their teams remotely. A study by Culture Wizard reports that "85 percent of global corporate leaders don't believe they've been successful in leading their virtual teams. The biggest challenges according to respondents were difficulty in communication, managing conflict, and building relationships. At a time when so many organizations say that the shift to remote teams will be permanent, this poses a major challenge to leaders." (Kruse, 2021)

Now is the time to do the development work to ensure you are ready to take on these and other challenges that occur in times of crisis. Crisis can shift a leader's environment quickly and no matter what, leaders need to be ready to tackle whatever challenges present themselves. The world is only becoming more fast paced, more connected, and more distraction filled. The way forward is with exceptional leadership, and those that step up to the plate will get the rewards, not just financially, but emotionally too. When you can lead others well, it will fill you up in a way that few roles will, and now is the time to become more deeply connected to your work.

WHY NOW RECAP

- Burnout is an occupational phenomenon that is defined as emotional exhaustion plus disillusionment plus withdrawal.
- Burnout affects 76 percent of workers at some time.
- Mental illnesses like depression and anxiety at all-time highs.
- Remote work is likely here to stay, and many leaders are struggling to lead their teams remotely.
- Doing work on your own leadership skills right now will help prepare you for the crises that you'll inevitably face as a leader.

CHAPTER 3

WHAT IS LEADERSHIP?

"Do not follow where the path may lead. Go instead where there is no path and leave a trail."

—HAROLD R. MCALINDON

In this as in all things, it's good to start at the beginning with what the heck leadership is and why you would want to do it. Definitions vary. Oxford Dictionary defines a leader as "the person who leads or commands a group, organization, or country." Merriam-Webster defines a leader as simply "something that leads." Is that people? A horse? Who knows? Is leadership a position? Are you a leader if you have a certain title?

One of my favorite leadership researchers and authors Simon Sinek says, "Leadership is not a rank. While there are people that have authority, that does not make them a leader. There are people who have no authority, but they themselves are leaders. We call them leaders because they go first. They take the risk before anyone else does. They choose to sacrifice so that their people may be safe and protected."

When I spoke with Heather Haas, ADVISA president and leadership consultant, she agreed. "I think the really excellent leaders are the ones who step up and figure out how to make it work. They support their colleagues and find ways to keep people connected, and that has nothing to do with job title."

Sometimes we associate leadership with management, but they are very different concepts. Management is associated with tasks like signing off on time sheets and writing performance evaluations. It's important, but it's not leadership.

Leadership consultant Mark Ferrara says, "What leaders do is they create a sense of vision that is so clear that people can act in their absence. They create alignment toward that vision, and then they motivate and inspire people, not as a group, but individually."

My favorite definition of leadership is Sheryl Sandberg's. She says, "Leadership is about making others better as a result of your presence and making sure that impact lasts in your absence." There are many methodologies and theories as to the best way to lead others, but the most effective for both employees and organizations is a servant or service leadership approach.

The terms "Servant Leadership" and "Service Leadership" are thrown around often, and I want to unpack what those actually are and what it means to live up to those ideals. I'd like to note that the two terms mean the same thing. Recently, the preferred language has shifted to "Service Leadership" because of increased awareness and sensitivity to the history of servants. I'll be using the term service from this point forward unless I'm directly quoting someone else.

The phrase "servant leadership" was first coined by Robert K. Greenleaf in The Servant as Leader, an essay that he first published in 1970. In that essay, Greenleaf said, "The servant-leader is servant first… It begins with the natural feeling that one wants to serve, to serve first. Then conscious choice brings one to aspire to lead. That person is sharply different from one who is leader first, perhaps because of the need to assuage an unusual power drive or to acquire material possessions."

Service Leadership starts with making sure you got into the job for the right reasons. Not because of a desire for power, but to help others.

When this model is put into action, Greenleaf said, "The difference manifests itself in the care taken by the servant—first to make sure that other people's highest priority needs are being served. The best test, and least difficult to administer, is:

- Do those served grow as persons?
- Do they, while being served, become healthier, wiser, freer, more autonomous, more likely themselves to become servants?
- And, what is the effect on the least privileged in society? Will they benefit or at least not be further deprived?"

A service-oriented leader's goal should be to empower others and put their needs first and foremost to help people develop and perform at their highest level. But this isn't just a squishy, touchy feely concept. It gets organizations massive results. When they are led by service-oriented leaders, "employees feel more engaged and purpose-driven, which in turn increases the organization's retention and lowers turnover costs. Well-trained and trusted staffers continue to develop as future leaders, thus helping to ensure the long-term viability of the organization." (Tarallo, 2021)

Southwest Airlines is a great example of this practice. Herb Kelleher was the cofounder, later CEO, and chairman emeritus of Southwest Airlines until his passing in 2019. The culture he created put employees first and customers second and led to an unheard of forty-seven-year streak of profitability that was just finally broken in 2020 as travel restrictions wreaked havoc on the airline industry. (Wolfsteller, 2021)

Kelleher's philosophy of "putting employees first resulted in a highly engaged, low-turnover workforce." (Tarallo, 2021) What did putting employees first look like? Southwest employees are empowered to do the right thing for the customer, and they trust their employees to do just that. Employees are held to a high standard and have clear expectations for what success looks like in their role. They also believe that when employees are treated well it translates to them having more passion for their work and that passion is then felt by the customer. (Morella-Olso, 2021)

His commitment to growing people has no greater success story than former Southwest CEO Colleen Barrett. As Kelleher became the company's chairman in 1978, he brought his longtime aide Colleen Barrett with him, and together they grew Southwest Airlines from a Texas carrier to a major airline. Barrett went on to be Kelleher's successor as CEO. (Johnson, 2017)

So why aren't there more service-oriented leaders in the world? I think our culture has a lot to do with that issue. We just don't see it in action in our lives or even in the media we consume. In so many movies that depict a workplace and a boss, you see disengaged employees led by someone who is either all command and control or completely incompetent. My favorite example is the cult classic *Office Space.* The main character, Peter's, boss is Bill Lumbergh. Bill is both clueless and incompetent and delights in enacting ineffective processes, bothering employees by dropping by unannounced, and giving them no notice that they need to work extra hours, including weekends. The workers are so disengaged that Peter and a few coworkers decide to skim money from the company. Things get so out of hand, the building eventually burns down, TPS reports and all.

Examples of good leadership in film are often portrayed by sports coaches. My favorite of this genre is *Remember the Titans*, which is based on a true story. Denzel Washington plays Coach Herman Boone, who was hired to coach the first integrated football team in Alexandria, Virginia. Coach Boone's combination of tough love and drive for results helps the team come together to become an undefeated football team that rallies the community right along with them. But this isn't a perfect leadership example either. Several scenes, including one that takes place in the middle of the night as the boys run to the Gettysburg battlefield, make you question Coach Boone's methods. You see his true heart by the end of the movie, but it takes a bit to get there.

I use the word heart intentionally. Leadership is all heart. Leadership is at its best when it's about the employees and the team and not the leader. Its energy comes from the humans. People with lives, families, career ambitions, and heartache. Ignore any of those, and you've got a recipe for disaster.

Service-oriented leadership needs to be demonstrated often, not just through words but through actions and behaviors. In my experience developing and coaching leaders, there are seven competencies that, when developed, lead to effective service-oriented leadership. Here are the seven competencies:

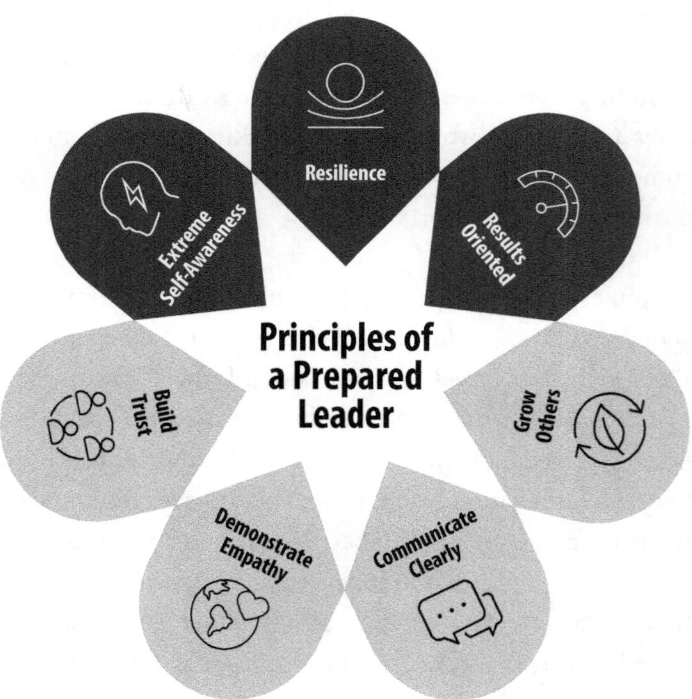

When you develop these competencies in advance of crisis, you will be able to lead through them as effectively as possible. I call them the principles of prepared leadership. In the following chapters, we will deep dive into each of these areas, and I'll give you tips not just for how to build the skills and behaviors in normal circumstances, but also give you best practices for tweaking these principles when crisis occurs. Before crisis hits, you need to have leadership practices already in place.

As you navigate the rest of the book, it will be helpful to do a quick self-assessment on these key behaviors. Use the activity here to get a baseline of your current skills. This is intended to be a fast assessment of your skills and isn't based on a scientific evaluation of the data. However, it will give you an idea of where you might want to spend time building skill.

SELF-ASSESSMENT

Activity: How often are the below statements true for you?
Give yourself a score of 1-5 for each question. 1=Never, 2=Rarely,
3=Sometimes, 4=Often, 5=Always

	1	2	3	4	5
1. Regularly admit my mistakes.					
2. Take responsibility for what goes right and what goes wrong.					
3. Seek to understand the perspective of others.					
4. Communicate information appropriately to the team.					
5. Know what I do well and what I struggle with at work.					
6. Know my most important values.					
7. Regularly get enough sleep.					
8. Eat in a way that fuels my energy.					
9. Regularly move my body in a way that helps relieve stress.					
10. Willing to have tough conversations.					
11. Know what to say to others when they experience hard times.					
12. Know what to do when others experience hard times.					
13. Encourage employees to learn and grow new skills.					
14. Regularly learn new things.					
15. Help others navigate burnout.					

Score of 50-75: More often than not, you are demonstrating the principles of prepared leadership. Look at the questions you scored lowest in. Do you notice any trends? Are they related to the same topic? What keeps you from demonstrating these behaviors more often?

Score of 25-49: You are sometimes demonstrating the principles of prepared leadership, but something is holding you back. That could be time, energy, or a lack of training. Pick two or three behaviors that you scored low in and think about how you could start to demonstrate those behaviors more often. What would the value of that be to you and your team? What do you need to learn more about?

Score of 0-24: You are rarely demonstrating principles of prepared leadership. Organizational culture could be playing a role in how you are currently leading. What leadership behaviors do you see at work instead of the ones above? How might the culture you work in be affecting your behavior? What trends do you notice in your scores? Start small by picking two or three behaviors that you are demonstrating and pick up the frequency. How can you build these behaviors into your day-to-day interactions with your team?

WHAT IS LEADERSHIP RECAP:

- "Leadership is about making others better as a result of your presence and making sure that impact lasts in your absence."—Sheryl Sandburg
- Leadership is different than management.
- Anyone can be a leader, regardless of position or title.

- Service-Oriented Leadership is an effective way to lead others that will increase employee engagement and create cultures that thrive, even in times of crisis.
- Service-Oriented Leadership needs to be demonstrated. It can't just be lip service.
- The Principles of Prepared Leadership will help you on your path. They are extreme self-awareness, resilience, results-oriented, build trust, demonstrate empathy, communicate clearly and grow others.

PRINCIPLES OF A PREPARED LEADER (YOU)

INTRODUCTION

"Yesterday I was clever, so I wanted to change the world. Today, I am wise, so I am changing myself."

—RUMI

If you want to lead teams of engaged and productive employees, you have to start by examining yourself. Who you are as a person is exactly who you will be as a leader. If empathy comes easily to you in your personal relationships, then it likely will come easily for you as a leader. If you struggle with tough conversations in your personal relationships, then you likely will as a leader too. That's why if you want to improve your leadership skills, you have to start with the behaviors that are most important for you to understand about yourself.

Understanding who you are is critical to leadership success. Many scholars in fact believe it's the most important skill for leaders to develop. That's why we are starting with this group of principles. In this section of the book, you'll learn more about having extreme self-awareness, resilience, and results orientation.

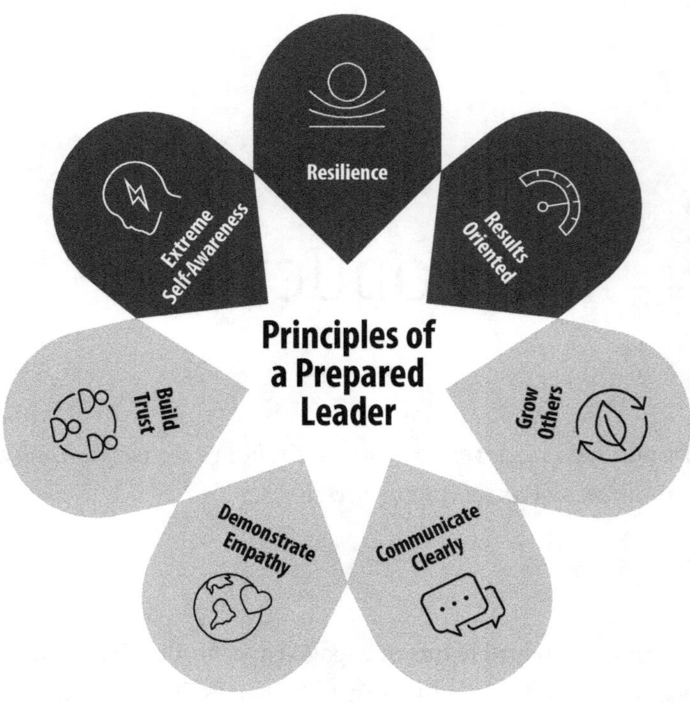

To build skill in any of these areas, you'll need to be willing to look inside and peel back the layers to get to who you are at your core. Each of these chapters includes exercises and reflection questions that will help you gain clarity about why you do what you do, what you value, how resilient you really are, and how you get the best results. It will be important to stop reading and complete the activities as you go through the chapters. Keep a notebook handy to make that easier.

You can also find printable worksheets of many of the activities on my website. Just go to *www.RashleighConsulting.com/Book* to grab a copy.

As you dig into understanding yourself better, it can be helpful to understand your strengths and weaknesses, your personality make-up, and your behavioral preferences. The marketplace is full of really great tools that you can access to get an unbiased look at yourself. However, be mindful of free internet assessments. Many are based on pseudoscience or were created as more of a scam than a true tool. It's best to work with a professional who can give you access to well researched and validated assessments.

A few I would recommend are the StrengthsFinder assessment, DISC behavioral assessment, and the Myers-Briggs Type Indicator (MBTI). Many larger corporations provide these assessments at no cost to employees, so ask around your workplace if that's of interest to you. If you can't get an assessment for free, you can search the internet for the assessment types and find a list of providers. You can also reach out to me directly, and I'm happy to help or make a recommendation.

With all that said, let's dig in and uncover who you are as a leader!

CHAPTER 4

EXTREME SELF-AWARENESS

—

"We cannot change what we are not aware of, and once we are aware, we cannot help but change."

—SHERYL SANDBERG

When you think of the qualities that make someone an exceptional leader, what comes to mind? This is a question I ask in my classes all the time. Every list that has ever been created includes self-awareness. Why is that?

Self-awareness is the single most important predictor of leadership success. Without it you may excel for a while, but at some point in your career, one of your blind spots will be your undoing.

I've seen it happen too many times, even to very high-level leaders. In a previous job, I once had an executive leader show up to a dinner held for high-potential leaders. These were leaders identified as being likely to move up the ranks of the organization. They were in town for a targeted development program, and the executive leader was there to meet everyone and stress the importance of the training they were undertaking. Unfortunately, he showed up to the event, had too much to drink, and then gave an extremely ineffective speech all about himself. Obviously, this was not the event kick-off I was hoping for, and I was not surprised to hear that this individual was asked to leave the organization a few months later. His lack of self-awareness was highlighted that evening.

Leaders who demonstrate extreme self-awareness know who they are, why they do what they do, and what they value.

KNOW YOURSELF

To be self-aware you have to know yourself. This starts with understanding what you do well and what you totally suck at. You don't have to know everything, and it is perfectly okay to have areas of weakness as a leader. That knowledge will help guide you as a leader and also sends a powerful message to your team. By understanding that you can't and don't know everything, you open yourself up to new ideas and information. Great leaders are great learners.

Self-awareness starts with mindset. Carol Dweck's research on mindset has been the gold standard for growth and development for years. It shows that a "fixed mindset assumes that our character, intelligence, and creative ability are static givens which we can't change in any meaningful way, and success is the affirmation of that inherent intelligence, an assessment of how those givens measure up against an equally fixed standard; striving for success and avoiding failure at all costs become a way of maintaining the sense of being smart or skilled."

However, people with a growth mindset "thrive on challenge and see failure not as evidence of unintelligence but as a heartening springboard for growth and for stretching our existing abilities. Out of these two mindsets, which we manifest from a very early age, springs a great deal of our behavior, our relationship with success and failure in both professional and personal contexts, and ultimately our capacity for happiness."

Reflection Activity: Make a list of ten of your biggest strengths. What do you consistently get positive feedback on? What do you really enjoy doing? What are your favorite parts of your job? That's where you'll find your strengths. Now, do the same with your weaknesses. What type of tasks do you find yourself avoiding? What are some areas that you've received constructive feedback on in the past? Those are your weaknesses. Once you've made your lists, show it to someone you trust to give you some honest feedback. Ask them what you've missed. Revise your list as needed.

Self-awareness is not a one and done task. You can be incredibly self-aware one day and then develop a new blind spot the next. You need practices in place to reflect regularly. To increase your self-awareness, there are some simple steps you can take. My advice? Take them. Often.

Start with daily reflection. What went really well today? What were some things that happened that were a mess? When were you stressed? How were your interactions with others? You can write down your answers in a notebook or computer file or even leave yourself a daily voicemail. The reflection is what is important, not the method. By asking yourself a few consistent reflection questions daily, you'll notice patterns. You might notice for three days in a row you've had tough interactions with your boss. What might the cause of that be? Maybe you need to have a bigger conversation with them.

Once you are reflecting regularly, move onto mentoring relationships. These could be formal or informal. Who can you count on to give you some regular, honest feedback? Who sees you interact with your team regularly? Form a relationship with them where you can seek their feedback on a regular basis. They can help illuminate blind spots and reinforce things you are doing well. Their feedback can be invaluable.

I had a leader who once gave me feedback that I needed to work on my poker face in meetings. I was shocked to learn that when others spoke, my opinion of their thoughts was clearly conveyed through my facial expressions. It was a true blind spot for me. Once I became aware of it, I was able to become more conscious of the behavior and adapt accordingly. I've never completely overcome this weakness but the awareness has been key!

VALUES

"The world is full of leaders with strong opinions and weak values. What if we strive for the opposite: strong values and

weak opinions? Integrity depends on being consistent in your principles. Progress depends on being flexible in your policies."
Adam Grant

The best leaders know what's most important to them and use that knowledge as a litmus test for their decision making. Your values can't be vague. They can't just be "do the right thing." They have to be based on deep knowledge and reflection about what's most important to you.

Remember Monica Cepero, the Broward County Deputy Commissioner who had to make some tough decisions about COVID-19 patients stuck on cruise ships? Why did she make this decision? She made the decision that lined up with her value of taking care of others, even when it wasn't popular.

As Brené Brown says in *Dare to Lead*, "A value is a way of being or believing that we hold most important. Living into our values means that we do more than profess our values, we practice them. We walk our talk—we are clear about what we believe and hold important and we take care that our intentions, words, thoughts and behaviors align with those beliefs."

Activity: *Use the values list provided to identify your top five values, or feel free to add your own. Then take it a step further and choose just two from your list of five. Once you've gotten to those two values ask yourself these questions:*

- *Are these words a reflection of who I am at my core?*
- *When I'm at my best, would these words describe me?*
- *Will these words help me make hard decisions?*

- *Would someone else be able to list these values based on my behavior?*

If the answer is not yes to all four, keep editing until it is.

VALUES LIST

Abundance	Competence	Flexibility
Accuracy	Confidence	Focus
Accountability	Continuous	Fortitude
Accomplishment	Conviction	Friendship
Adventure	Cooperation	Fun
Advocacy	Courage	Generosity
Agility	Courtesy	Goodness
Altruism	Creativity	Grace
Ambition	Credibility	Gratitude
Appreciation	Curiosity	Growth
Autonomy	Daring	Happiness
Awareness	Desire	Hard Work
Balance	Determination	Health
Beauty	Discovery	Honesty
Belonging	Diversity	Honor
Bliss	Drive	Humor
Boldness	Duty	Imagination
Bravery	Education	Inclusiveness
Brilliance	Effectiveness	Individuality
Camaraderie	Efficiency	Influence
Caring	Empathy	Inner Peace
Charity	Encouragement	Innovation
Charm	Enthusiasm	Inspiration
Change	Ethics	Integrity
Collaboration	Excellence	Intelligence
Comfort	Excitement	Intimacy
Commitment	Fairness	Intuition
Communication	Faith	Investing
Community	Family	Joy
Compassion	Fitness	Justice

Kindness	Philanthropy	Speed
Leadership	Poise	Spirituality
Learning	Power	Spontaneity
Logic	Preservation	Stability
Love	Privacy	Strength
Loyalty	Professionalism	Success
Mastery	Progress	Supremacy
Maturity	Prosperity	Sympathy
Meaning	Punctuality	Teamwork
Merit	Purity	Thoughtfulness
Modesty	Quiet	Tolerance
Money	Relationships	Trust
Neatness	Resilience	Understanding
Openness	Respect	Unity
Opportunity	Responsibility	Utility
Optimism	Risk-Taking	Valor
Order	Safety	Variety
Outcome	Satisfaction	Vision
Orientation	Security	Warmth
Outstanding	Selflessness	Wealth
Service	Service	Winning
Passion	Simplicity	Wisdom
Peace	Sincerity	Wonder
Persuasiveness	Skill	Zeal

I've completed the values activity with easily thousands of leaders over the last ten years. I can promise you two things: One, this activity is hard. It will be hard to choose just five values, let alone just a few. Two, you'll be a different leader as a result of this activity.

Personally, I completed this activity for the first time in a classroom. One of my colleagues was teaching a values activity, and as I observed in the back, I decided to complete it myself. I kept have these five values on an index card on my desk for years.

1. Growth
2. Balance
3. Honesty
4. Hard work
5. Curiosity

This list served me well. I often used it to help me decide everything from how to best handle a conflict with a coworker to conversations about work life balance with my boss and family.

In November of 2018, a friend and I decided to take a girl's trip to Austin, Texas, to hear the amazing Brené Brown speak in person. Her book, *Dare to Lead*, was just launching, and she was speaking to promote the book. We sat transfixed for over an hour as she spoke.

As part of the conversation, she asked us all if we could name our top two values and gave us some space to think about them. Right there, in that room, I was able to quickly identify my top two values within moments: hope and curiosity. Here's what they mean to me.

Curiosity is all about continuing to grow and learn. I don't ever want to be done learning, growing, and expanding. I don't want to assume I know the right answer. I want to ask questions that help myself and others solve hard problems.

Hope for me is all about the belief that things will work out just the way they should. I can look back on so many times in my life that seemed hopeless but each one of those times led me right to where I am now, helped me grow, and served as fuel when times got hard.

Now, how do I use these values to help me make decisions? Let's say I have a hypothetical employee on my team who's not performing well. I would start with getting curious about why. Instead of jumping to conclusions, I'd ask questions hoping that the root issue is one I can help resolve.

I often use hope as a litmus test on when to stay and leave situations. For instance, in a previous role, there was a major project that my team was asked to implement that I knew in my core was not right for the organization. I respectfully fought that decision until I no longer had hope that my voice was being heard. I then got curious about ways that I could help it succeed. After hitting brick wall after brick wall, it became clear that each of these values was in major conflict. I knew it was time to leave my role. That's the beauty of understanding what you value most. It helps make tough decisions easy.

YOUR WHY

Research from Career Builder shows that just 34 percent of American workers will take on a leadership role at some point in their career and only 7 percent aspire to take on Senior Leadership positions. The reasons why people aren't interested in the roles vary, but many are content in current roles and "slightly more than one third didn't want to suffer the diminished work-life balance perceived to be connected to leadership positions." (Salerno, 2014)

Leadership can be a difficult job. So why does anyone take it on? In the book *The Motive* by Patrick Lencioni, he makes the case that there are only two reasons people become a leader. The first is "to do whatever you need to do to serve the people." The second is because "they want to be rewarded." He argues that fewer people should be leaders because too many people are getting into the job because of the rewards instead of to serve. Effective leaders know why they got into leadership, and it's not for the pay or the power, it's to help and serve others.

Like so many others, I accidentally became a leader. In my first "real job" after college as a recruiter, I was responsible for managing and leading our human resources assistant. I don't honestly think that part of the role was even discussed in the job description or in the interview process. I was neither ready nor capable of leading another person at that time. Frankly, I did a bad job at it. I was terrible at leadership basics like clear communication and expectation setting and even more terrible at setting boundaries. That translated to an often confused and overworked employee, and a struggle with an overtime budget that I couldn't seem to keep in check.

As I grew into my future leadership roles, I became clearer and clearer about my purpose as a leader. My goal was to help people be as successful as they could for themselves and the organization. With that in my mind, I behaved very differently. I was more likely to communicate regularly with my team and set them up for success. I got to know them better as people and did my best to demonstrate that they could trust me. And I had much better outcomes both for the organizations I worked for and for my team members.

In his book, *Start with Why,* Simon Sinek points out that everyone in an organization knows "WHAT" they do. Some know "HOW" they do it. But very few know "WHY" they do what they do. He points out that the reason can't be to make a profit. That's a result, and it will always be a result of providing something of value.

This is true for leaders as well. Your results will be directly related to your why. As Sinek asks, "What's your purpose? What's your cause? What's your belief? Why does your organization exist? Why do you get out of the bed in the morning and why should anyone care?"

And as Lencioni says, "Why be a leader? If your why is off, then the how won't matter!"

During my time with the government, I often worked for leaders who were in the role just to be eligible for their next promotion. One of the worst offenders was an officer I worked with for about a year. I had been in my role for about six months and was a part of a small team that was creating a brand-new leadership development curriculum for the organization. My role was very high profile, and I often interacted with him.

One afternoon, I heard him walking down the hall. It sounded like he was stopping in each office along the way and chatting with the office occupant. To say this was unusual would be a huge understatement. He very rarely left his office. As he came into my office to chat with me, he stepped back outside my door to look at my nameplate, then said "Hey Beth! How are things going?" As you can imagine, I didn't have much to share with him. He didn't even remember my name! In theory, he was doing something I advise a lot of leaders to do: checking in and connecting with his team members. But because his "why" was so misaligned, that behavior didn't matter and honestly did more harm than good.

Activity: Reflect back on your first leadership position. What appealed to you about the role? Why did you pursue it? What difference did you make in your team's life? How is being a leader connected to your values? What about leadership is appealing to you? What kind of impact do you want to make on others? Think about your why. Then create a leadership philosophy.

A leadership philosophy can be both aspirational and inspirational but should be grounded in who you are at your core. Think about your values. How do they impact who you are as a leader? What characteristics do you want to embody? The final form of the philosophy can vary. Get creative. What will be inspirational for you?

It could be a statement like this:

"I am in my role to serve others, help them grow, and help them reach their full potential both in their role and in their life."

Or a visual like this:

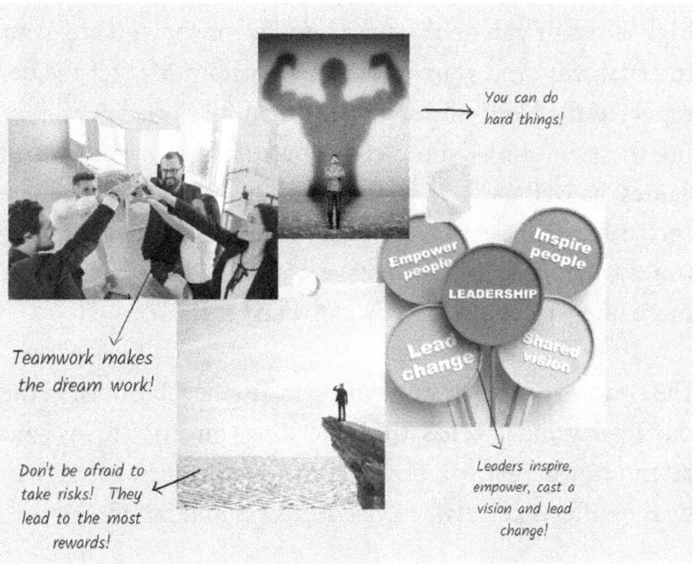

Or even a quote that inspires you like:

"Leaders must be close enough to relate to others, but far enough ahead to motivate them." John C. Maxwell

Once you've created your leadership philosophy, keep it close to you to remind yourself why you got into this line of work. It's not for the weak at heart. In times of crisis, knowing why you are in a leadership position will matter. This activity can be even more powerful when you pair it with a strong understanding of what you value.

CRISIS APPLICATION

Why focus on self-awareness now? Because any strengths and weaknesses you have will be amplified in times of crisis and high stress. If you don't have a handle on who you are, your internal why, and your values, it will show. Market Insider reported that "self-aware people are more skilled at regulating their emotions, more conscious of their priorities and values, as well as their strengths and weaknesses. To have such a deep connection to self is powerful, especially during times when people's thoughts, emotions, and behaviors are more likely to be clouded by panic and fear."

The clearer you are on what you bring to the table both in the day-to-day and in crisis, the better able you are to focus your attention where it will best serve you and your team. It can be the difference between crisis success and failure.

EXTREME SELF-AWARENESS RECAP

- Leaders who demonstrate extreme self-awareness know who they are, why they do what they do, and what they value.
- Leaders are learners. Adopting a growth mindset is critical to leadership success.
- Know what your strengths and weaknesses are and have feedback channels in place to be sure you don't miss blind spots.
- Understand why you want to be a leader. Writing a leadership philosophy statement can help ground you in your motive.
- Know your values and use them as a litmus test for decision making.

CHAPTER 5

RESILIENCE

—

"A good half of the art of living is resilience."
—ALAIN DE BOTTON

Resilience both in the day-to-day and in times of crisis is critical to happiness and success. However, some interesting new research shows that most people overestimate how much resilience they have. Everyday Health reported that 83 percent of Americans polled believed that they had high levels of resilience when only 57 percent of people actually did.

Resilience at its core is all about how we bounce back from adversity—how we get up, dust ourselves off, and get back to work on our most important goals. If we were to examine historical times of crisis, we would see that resilience has been the difference maker when it comes to crisis management. Those with the highest resilience skills have fared the best, but we have to pull off our rose-colored glasses to get a true picture of how resilient we really are so we can learn and grow where needed.

We tend to focus more on resilience in times of stress. However, stress isn't always a bad thing. Research shows "that people who believe stress can be a benefit do a better job of handling challenges. We can experience positive benefits, even under extreme stress. These effects are simply more likely to occur when people are in a mindset that orients them that way." (Sanders, 2020)

Resilience is important for both small stuff, like a bad traffic jam that makes you late for work, and for big stuff like illness, heartbreak, and global pandemics. If our resilience is low, even small setbacks can feel like complete disasters. It takes us considerable time to get back on our feet when we fall down due to the ebbs and flow of life. But if our resilience is higher, we can bounce back more quickly from setbacks and use those situations as an opportunity to grow. (Rossouw, 2017)

Many scholars and researchers work in the resilience field, but my favorite research comes from the Driven company in Australia. Their model accounts not just for the typical resilience factors, but they've also conducted deep research on how our health affects our resilience. Especially when it comes to reducing burnout, I think this is an essential inclusion. (Rossouw, 2017)

The Driven Model of Resilience is made of six domains: vision, composure, collaboration, reasoning, tenacity, and health. Each of these factors in combination makes up our overall resilience. (Rossouw, 2017) There may be some areas that are easy for you and some that are a struggle; that's perfectly normal. However, resilience can be improved by anyone who is willing to do the work. As we dig into each of these domains, I'll give you some action items for improving in that area. Doing the work will help you take off your rose-colored glasses and ensure that you don't fall into the trap of overestimating your resilience.

VISION

The vision domain is about purpose and meaning. Do you have goals and plans that drive you? Are you able to work and make progress on your most meaningful goals? When we have a clear vision, it motivates us to act. All six domains of resilience are important, but vision is most important because it serves as a guidepost for any of the changes you might want to make in the other domains.

In times of crisis, it can be difficult to stay on track with meaningful goals. That can happen due to lack of time or energy as burnout becomes real. At the beginning of 2020, I decided to try a new yearly goal setting method. I set twenty goals that I wanted to accomplish in 2020. There were big goals and small ones. Here's that list:

1) Find a health coach that I enjoy working with.
2) Take five family vacations.
3) Take two girls' trips.
4) Weekend away with just Matt.
5) Take Sam on a summer adventure, just the two of us.
6) Walk in a 5K.
7) Book five speaking gigs.
8) Perfect my keynote.
9) Write fifty thousand words towards a book.

10) Take two personal retreats.

11) Go on five family hikes.

12) Get family photos taken.

13) Hire a virtual assistant.

14) Build a mastermind group that I want to participate in.

15) Create a resource that helps others start their business.

16) Read fifty books and track them.

17) Have a monthly lunch date with Mom.

18) Attend a business conference.

19) Launch a course.

20) Create at least one passive income source.

But then the global pandemic hit. I look back at this list now and chuckle. Beth in 2019 was so sweet. She thought she was going to get to travel. How about instead, I'll spend more time at home than any human should ever spend? How about instead of getting more quality time with my parents, I won't be able to see them indoors for six months? I can laugh about it now.

As the pandemic settled in, and I realized most of these goals wouldn't happen, I lost direction. In an effort to motivate myself in the fall, I started to take note of what goals I had accomplished that weren't on that list. They included:

1) Becoming a certified resilience coach.

2) Receiving my ACC coaching certification.

3) Taught sixth grade to my son.

4) Pivoted my business and kept it running in the middle of a pandemic.

5) Moved into our dream house.

6) Spent some of the best quality time I've ever spent with Matt and Sam.

7) Rested.

8) Spoke virtually at a National Conference and an awards ceremony.

9) Helped several clients move training and development efforts from in-person to virtual.

10) Survived.

I also took a hard look at the intention behind my original list. I was craving quality time with the people in my life. I usually find that when I'm on vacation or adventures with people, but it turns out, I can get that time at home too. I just have to slow down enough to allow for it.

ACTION ITEMS

- *If you aren't in the habit of setting goals for yourself, start. For most people, having something to work towards is incredibly helpful and will drive you when things get hard.*

- *If things don't go the way you think they will, adjust. Set new goals. Reassess and look for ways to pivot. Find new sources of meaning and purpose and set new goals that will help you feel fulfilled. Every goal, whether achieved or not, leads to the next goal and experience.*

- *Activities like knowing your values and your leadership philosophy are also great ways to cast a vision for your life and work. Be sure to complete them if you haven't already!*

COMPOSURE

The composure domain is about our ability to regulate our emotions. Composure also helps us recognize the signs of stress and anxiety and helps us manage them. A big part of this factor is first recognizing that you are having an emotion, knowing what it is, and what to do to regulate it.

The best leaders know how to regulate and process their emotions. Composure is a key element of emotional intelligence and executive presence because it helps those around you feel calm and inspires confidence. But keeping your composure in the face of crisis can be difficult. (Overby, 2019)

If you struggle with composure, there are some tangible things you can do to help. It can be helpful to think of emotions as information instead of directions for what our behavior should look like. For example, if I start to feel angry in a meeting because I don't feel that my voice is being heard, I can notice that and then choose to pause and reflect on why that might make me angry. Are my values being challenged? Do I feel a lack of respect? By pausing to gain clarity I can now choose my behavior differently. I might choose to express it very differently based on that reflection.

ACTION ITEMS

- *Start noticing when you are experiencing an emotion. Take a deep breath and notice how you are feeling. Are you sad? Mad? Frustrated? Hungry? Just recognizing that something is happening inside your body is the first step to changing it. If this doesn't come easily, I highly recommend keeping a feelings wheel (Wilcox, 1982) somewhere you can see it. It can help you build your emotional language.*

- *Try re-framing a common emotion. For instance, nervousness and excitement cause many of the same physical responses in our bodies. Your hands might get sweaty. You might pace. Your heart rate increases. When you notice those physical signs, re-frame those nerves as excitement.*
- *Do you know what helps you feel less stressed? Is it a nap? Is it a phone call with a friend? Is it a walk or run? Knowing what helps reduce your stress and then acting on it when you feel stress will help you increase your composure. Once you know what reduces stress you can also start to complete those activities proactively. Are you getting ready to have a difficult conversation? Take a walk before the call. It will help you start at a more neutral state.*

COLLABORATION

The collaboration domain involves the critical need of the human brain to have close and secure relationships with others. Having a support network of friends, colleagues, and even pets can have an effect on our overall resilience. This factor is also about our ability to relate to others and form connections. We need meaningful collaboration with others to reach our full potential.

Collaboration is typically an area that comes naturally to me. I truly enjoy strong relationships with others, especially my core support network. But the pandemic turned collaboration into something I had to work hard to find. As the world locked down, suddenly lunch with a friend wasn't an option and my support network became just my husband, son, and dogs. Loneliness became an issue for many, including me. I found myself longing for simple things like working at my local Starbucks with the noise around me, grabbing a pedicure with my mom or a friend, and even our neighborhood game night tradition.

Collaboration had to become intentional. I leaned hard into technology tools and scheduled Zoom calls with friends and colleagues. I also literally started scheduling check-in time blocks on my calendar where I would call or text friends and family to check in. It helped, a little. But there is truly no replacement for in-person connection. You can't hug someone on Zoom and people are so much less likely to be real about their life through that medium.

If collaboration isn't something that comes easily for you, or if like me, you've struggled with it while under extreme stress or in crisis situations, there are some actionable steps you can take.

ACTION ITEMS

- *Mentors can be incredibly helpful for developing your collaboration skills. You can learn both from the other person's experiences and the natural collaboration from the relationship will also help you grow.*
- *Think about other people that you feel collaborate well. What do they do? What actions do they take? How do they make you feel when you interact with them? Try out a few of their techniques.*
- *Schedule time for collaboration. The pace of life can make it easy to shift collaboration to a low priority. Intentionally schedule time to connect with others and build relationships. It won't happen by accident.*

REASONING

The reasoning domain is all about how we use our critical thinking skills to solve problems. To do this most successfully we have to be able to think clearly during times of stress and use our resources wisely. Individuals with high reasoning skills also have the ability to recognize their thinking style and manage any blind spots that they encounter.

Thinking style has a lot to do with how much information we like to consider before making a decision. Do you like to spend time analyzing data or talking to knowledgeable people about an issue, or do you tend to be able to trust your own instincts and decide quickly? Both thinking styles can be effective but understanding which you prefer will help you know how to counteract potential issues.

For instance, I'm someone who tends to make decisions quickly from my gut and that thinking style tends to serve me well. However, I've learned over the years that I sometimes skip the step of explaining why I made the decision I did with my team. That's something I've worked on over the years and it helps me manage the potential downside of my quick-to-act thinking style.

If you want to increase your reasoning ability there are some tactical things you can do.

ACTION ITEMS

- *Identify potential problems before they happen. Think about three major things that could happen for your team. What are they? What would you do to solve them if they happen? This type of proactive planning will help you act quickly if the problem occurs.*

- *Get in the habit of thinking of multiple solutions to problems. We often tend to act once we come up with a solution but instead challenge ourselves to come up with three options. What are the pros and cons of each? Which is the cheapest? Which will have the biggest risks? This process will help you come to a better solution and slow you down so you can engage your critical thinking skills.*

- *If you are someone who tends to struggle to come up with multiple solutions, look for people around you to brainstorm with during times of crisis. Who can help you think outside the box on how to solve critical issues?*

TENACITY

The tenacity domain is about perseverance. How do we bounce back from setbacks? How do we learn from our own successes and experience? Research shows that perseverance is more important than intelligence in achieving success. (Rossouw, 2017)

I like to call this the "scrappy" factor. Are you willing to claw your way to your goals if needed? For some reason when I think of tenacity I always think about professional athletes or Olympians. They are people who are willing to work incredibly hard, push through injury and work towards a goal that is highly unlikely to come true have tenacity. People with high tenacity also have a realistic sense of hope. They aren't overly optimistic or pessimistic, but they are willing to continue to do hard things when challenged.

If you want to increase your tenacity, you can with a few activities.

ACTION ITEMS

- *Reflect on mistakes. What can you learn when something goes wrong so that you handle things differently next time? This isn't about beating yourself up but truly using your reasoning ability to see where things went wrong, so you can adjust.*
- *Focus on learning, not judgment. Judgment can be hard to avoid. We all judge ourselves and others. Shift your focus from judging to learning. What's the lesson from the setback or situation?*
- *Know what you're willing to fight hard for in life and what you aren't. Sometimes we aren't tenacious because the goal isn't important to us. When that's the case, set the goal aside and focus on the things that really are important to you.*

HEALTH

The health domain is foundational. Taking care of ourselves supports a healthy brain and increases our ability to build resilience in all the other domains. The three areas of health that are measured are exercise, nutrition, and sleep. I've found that most people struggle in at least one of these areas. If you are exercising regularly, maybe you are sacrificing sleep. If you are focusing on sleep, maybe you aren't taking the time to prepare healthy meals. You want these three factors to work together in harmony.

If you want to do some work on your health, here are a few tips.

ACTION ITEMS

- *Focus on one area at a time. Which feels the most urgent or attainable? Start there with a mini goal. For example, if you are currently getting five hours of sleep, try for six. How does your body feel when you get that extra hour? Make it a habit before you move on to something else.*
- *Focus on activities that you enjoy. If you are like me and struggle to find the joy in exercise, do some experimenting. Maybe you hate running but would love to go to a Zumba class with a friend. Maybe you struggle to find time to go to the gym but can do a thirty-minute yoga class from your house.*
- *Look for ways to get help. If you struggle with healthy eating, would a meal planning service help? Would a personal trainer help you meet your goals? Would asking your partner to get up with kids or pets three nights a week help you meet your sleep goals? Ask for help if you need it!*

 *Reflection Activity: Now that you've learned about each of the factors that make up resilience, which ones need some extra attention? Choose two of these factors and complete the action items. By digging into these areas, you'll become a more effective and resilient leader.*

RESILIENCE RECAP

- Resilience is a blind spot for many as we often rate ourselves as more resilient than we really are in practice.
- Stress can be positive when we can see it as an opportunity.
- Resilience can be learned. You can get more resilient if you do the work.
- Resilience has six domains: vision, composure, collaboration, reasoning, tenacity, and health. Each of these factors in combination make up our overall resilience.

CHAPTER 6

RESULTS-ORIENTATED

"You don't get results by focusing on results. You get results by focusing on the actions that produce results."

—MIKE HAWKINS

Great leaders get results. They get results for the people they lead and for the organizations they are a part of because if they don't, they likely won't get to keep their leadership positions for long. But the way you get those results matters. Behaving as if everyone is simply a cog in a machine or a minion there to do your bidding won't inspire people to get things done. It will create resentful, disgruntled workers and teams.

It's the combination of a focus on results and social skills that lead to great leadership. *Harvard Business Review* reports that "if a leader was seen as being very strong on results focus, the chance of that leader being seen as a great leader was only 14 percent and if a leader was strong on social skills, he or she was seen as a great leader even less of the time—a paltry 12 percent. However, for leaders who were strong in both results focus *and* in social skills, the likelihood of being seen as a great leader skyrocketed to 72 percent."

So how many leaders out there are meeting this high bar? Less than 1 percent of leaders possess both high social skills and a focused goal.

Shocked? Me too. That number is surprisingly low and it got me thinking about why. I think the answer lies in the number of leaders who lack the ability to clearly set a goal and then hold someone accountable for that goal. Think about the mechanics of a feedback conversation. It's a combination of holding someone accountable for a goal or task and clearly and kindly communicating that the work isn't meeting the mark. How many leaders do you know that can walk that line?

The good news? If you can manage to do it, you'll be an incredibly successful leader.

In my last corporate role, I had a leader who did an exceptional job balancing social skills and getting results. She is incredibly focused on relationships with her direct reports, peers, and customers. She knew us all as people and built our trust in the day-to-day interactions we had with her. She is also incredibly willing to have tough conversations. She sets expectations and then holds people accountable to them.

She did two specific things that I really loved as a member of her team. The first was creating a true culture of feedback. She built feedback channels into the regular cadence of our day to day. Each team meeting started with positive feedback peer to peer. At the end of every one-on-one meeting, she asked for feedback and gave feedback, both positive and constructive. She modeled and lived the feedback culture, and it served our team well.

She also set incredibly clear expectations. She painted a picture of what success in our roles looked like and then she tracked our progress. In my role, I had the clearest expectations I've ever had in my career. Every part of my job had a metric associated with it and progress was tracked on a dashboard that was reviewed by the team each month. We could tell just by looking at a spreadsheet whether we were winning or losing. The combination of both components helped our team succeed and gain credibility with our customers and the organization as a whole.

GOAL SETTING

One of my favorite passages from *Alice in Wonderland* is:

"Would you tell me, please, which way I ought to go from here?"
"That depends a good deal on where you want to get to," said the Cat.
"I don't much care where—" said Alice.
"Then it doesn't matter which way you go," said the Cat.
"—so long as I get somewhere," Alice added as an explanation.
"Oh, you're sure to do that," said the Cat, "if you only walk long enough."

Unclear goals cause unnecessary confusion and rework. If you don't set a clear path for your team to travel down, they'll end up somewhere you don't want them to be. Setting clear goals and expectations is a critical part of leadership success.

There is a ton of research on how to set clear goals, but the method I recommend is from *The Four Disciplines of Execution*. That method recommends setting goals as a formula of "from x to y by when." I love it because it forces you to spell out both the current state and the goal. It also helps you write a goal that is clear enough to be tracked. For example, a car sales team may set a goal by saying, "Our team will sell a dozen vehicles by the end of the month." This example can be easily tracked and has a clear deadline. Anyone who reads it would know exactly what the goal means. That's what you want.

If possible, engage your employees in the goal setting process. They should have a clear voice in the process. Ask them, "What's something you think we need to be doing that we're not," or "What's a project you're excited to make progress on this year?" Then write the goals together with a clear eye on how the goal connects to the organization's mission. The more you can connect the two, the more effective your team will be at helping your company do well.

In one of my roles at the CIA, I had a leader who laid out for me how my goals were specifically connected to the greater mission of the agency. It's easy when you work in a support function at an organization with a big mission to lose sight of how you fit into that bigger picture. In the five years before, I never had a leader who was able to do that, and it changed how I felt about my work in an amazing way.

It's important not just to set a goal but to also track it in a compelling and easy way that can be regularly referenced and discussed. Without that tracking, it will be much harder for your employees to meet your expectations and you'll struggle to clearly communicate feedback when needed.

Once the goal is set, check in regularly with your employees in a systematic way. The goal here isn't to micromanage or under-manage but to walk the middle ground. A great way to do this is to agree on when and where check-ins will take place. Then stick to that schedule. Provide support and guidance as needed and be sure to praise all the amazing things that are happening.

GOAL SETTING PLANNER

Activity: Take a stab at writing a goal using the Goal Setting Planner. Then, share it with your employees.

WHAT DO YOU WANT TO MAKE PROGRESS ON?

WHAT'S THE CURRENT STATE OF THE EFFORT?

WHAT WILL SUCCESS LOOK LIKE? HOW WILL YOU KNOW
YOU'VE SUCCEEDED?

WRITE THE GOAL HERE (FROM X TO Y BY WHEN):

HOW WILL YOU TRACK THIS GOAL?

WHO DO YOU NEED TO SHARE THIS GOAL WITH?

FEEDBACK CONVERSATIONS

In my coaching practice, I easily spend 30-40 percent of my time helping leaders get prepared to have feedback conversations with their employees. It's one of my most common requests. Why? Usually one of three reasons:

1. No one has ever taught them how to have an effective feedback conversation and they have no idea what to do.
2. They've never experienced an effective feedback conversation themselves and don't realize that it can be done.
3. They are terrified of the employee's reaction.

These are all incredibly valid reasons to need help. Fortunately, this skill can and should be learned. Start by building a practice of preparing for the conversation. Take some time to think about what you want to say and how you want to say it. Think about how the other person might react. What's the best-case scenario? The worst case? What will you do if either happens? Use the worksheet I've provided here or find another by simply googling feedback planner. You'll find a ton of options that will work. The key is the preparation itself.

For years leadership training included the idea that feedback should be "sandwiched": one positive, a negative and then another positive piece of feedback. Unfortunately, it's terrible advice. Your employee will walk away completely confused by the conversation. My advice instead is to focus on framing the conversation with positive intent. That will communicate how much you value the employee and then you can provide your feedback. Too often we expect people to just inherently know why we are doing what we are doing or saying what we are saying. Take that guesswork out of the equation. Be transparent. Are you sharing the feedback because you truly care about their job success and this issue is standing in their way? Then tell them.

This could sound like: "Amy, I need to share some feedback with you. My intention in sharing it is to support you and help you be as successful as possible in your role. In last week's staff meeting you lost your temper, and it really affected the level of collaboration in the room. People stopped contributing ideas and we lost momentum on solving a critical problem. Tell me more about what was happening for you."

ENGAGING FEEDBACK CONVERSATION PLANNER

Activity: Use the feedback planner to get prepared for a conversation you've been avoiding. Then discuss your plan with a trusted friend, coach or mentor. Adjust your plan as needed, then go have the conversation. You'll be a better leader because of it!

WHO DO YOU NEED TO HAVE A CONVERSATION WITH?

WHAT HAVE YOU NOTICED? WHAT ARE THE OBSERVABLE FACTS?

WHAT'S THE IMPACT?

HOW WILL YOU START THE CONVERSATION?

WHAT QUESTIONS DO YOU WANT TO ASK?

HOW WILL YOU CLOSE THE CONVERSATION?

If you have fear or discomfort around having tough feedback conversations, welcome to the club! For many, many leaders, this fear keeps them from having conversations that need to happen. That fear grows exponentially if you have any tendencies towards people pleasing. Unfortunately, I know this from experience. I have the tendency to avoid tough conversations because I don't want other people to be upset or to dislike me. I've had to do deep internal work on my own hang-ups with tough conversations.

Two thought leaders helped me with my mindset around feedback conversations. The first was Kim Scott who wrote Radical Candor, a great book on how to build a culture of feedback within organizations. In that book, she shares the story of an employee who worked for her at Google. The employee was incredibly likable; the kind of guy who knew his coworkers well and went out of his way to build relationships. He was funny and kind. Sadly, he was also terrible at his job and Kim avoided feedback conversation with him because she liked him so much. The first time he received feedback on his performance was when she had to fire him due to gross incompetence. The poor guy was completely blindsided. The lesson? You aren't doing anyone a favor by withholding critical feedback. If an employee doesn't know there is a problem, they can't shift their behavior, learn something new, and get better.

The second was of course my hero Brené Brown. In Dare to Lead, she shares a mantra: "Clear is kind. Unclear is unkind." Sugarcoating doesn't do anyone any favors. You can't build trust with others when you are actively lying to them, and that's what you are doing when you don't share your honest opinion.

Both pieces of advice helped me shift my mindset around feedback. Feedback, when given well and with positive intent, is an incredible gift to be able to give to your team. It will help them be their very best.

The final thing that helped me reduce my fear was practice and experience. The more you willingly walk into tough conversations prepared to have them, the better you will get at it. This will happen even more quickly if you get lucky and have a few early wins. Today one of my favorite things in the world is giving someone feedback or a suggestion that they take and use to their advantage. I love watching other people succeed. If I can be a tiny part of that, why wouldn't I want to be?

Reflection Activity: What fears do you have around tough conversations? What ideas do you have about how you could start to overcome those fears? What helps you feel less anxious? How can you get nervous energy out ahead of the conversation? What might you be withholding that could be important for your employees to know?

CRISIS APPLICATION

Feedback and accountability play a critical role during times of crisis. They don't happen in isolation and more often than not, when a crisis occurs, someone saw it was coming and was trying to alert others. A great example of that is the space shuttle Challenger tragedy in January of 1986. That space shuttle exploded killing seven astronauts because the O-rings failed due to cold temperatures. The Report of the Presidential Commission on the Space Shuttle Challenger Accident showed that several engineers both at NASA and at the contractor Morton Thiokol had repeatedly alerted others that there were problems with the O-rings and that they expressed those concerns before the launch. (Klann, 2003)

Gene Klann, author and consultant for the Center for Creative leadership says, "The Challenger story is a dramatic example, but it's not unique. Often employees may have no reporting avenue, will not be listened to if they do report what they observe, or feel disconnected from the organization and therefore simply stand by and let the crisis unfold. This type of passive aggressive, negative behavior reflects on the leadership of the organization." He also says that the key to making sure employees can speak truth to power is "if the organization's leadership communicates clearly, builds relationships and connects emotionally, and highlights personal and organizational vision and values, then it is less likely that this kind of behavior will occur. These points are critical to preparing for a crisis." (Klann, 2003)

The lesson? Be sure that you have channels for employees to share their concerns with you and listen to them when they do. It will help you anticipate potential issues before they occur. By setting clear goals and then developing practices that allow for frequent feedback opportunities, you will create a culture where feedback is just what you and your team do. It's not new or scary. It's how the team gets better. It will help you get the results you and your organization need during times of crisis.

RESULT ORIENTED RECAP

- Great leaders use a combination of social skills and results focus to motivate and inspire others but less than one percent of current leaders can do both well.
- Create clear, trackable goals by using the formula "from x to y by when."
- Willingness to have a clear and kind feedback conversation is critical to leadership success.
- Use a feedback planner to ensure that you are well prepared for these conversations, especially if you have fear or anxiety about them.
- When big issues and problems occur, someone usually noticed them. Be sure to have channels in place for employees to share what they know. It can help you avoid many crisis situations.

PART 3

PRINCIPLES OF A PREPARED LEADER (YOUR TEAM)

INTRODUCTION

———

"A leader takes people where they want to go. A great leader takes people where they don't necessarily want to go, but ought to be."

—ROSALYNN CARTER

Now that you understand yourself better, we need to shift our focus to leading your team. Leading a team can be one of the most rewarding jobs in the world. But to do it well, you need to come into the role with a service-oriented mindset. Your job as a leader is to get results through other people and people are complex. You aren't leading machines that can be programmed to perform under perfect conditions. They will have hard days, get confused about tasks and expectations, and will rely on you to help them grow and improve.

There are four principles that when used, will help you lead your team to exceptional results.

We will start by exploring trust because without trust as a base, the other principles will be very difficult to implement. Then we'll move into the skill that can take your leadership to the next level—the ability to show empathy to others. We will dig into some really fascinating research that shows just how important this skill set is to your leadership success. Finally, I'll give you some tips and tricks for communicating clearly and continuing to develop your team members, especially during times of crisis.

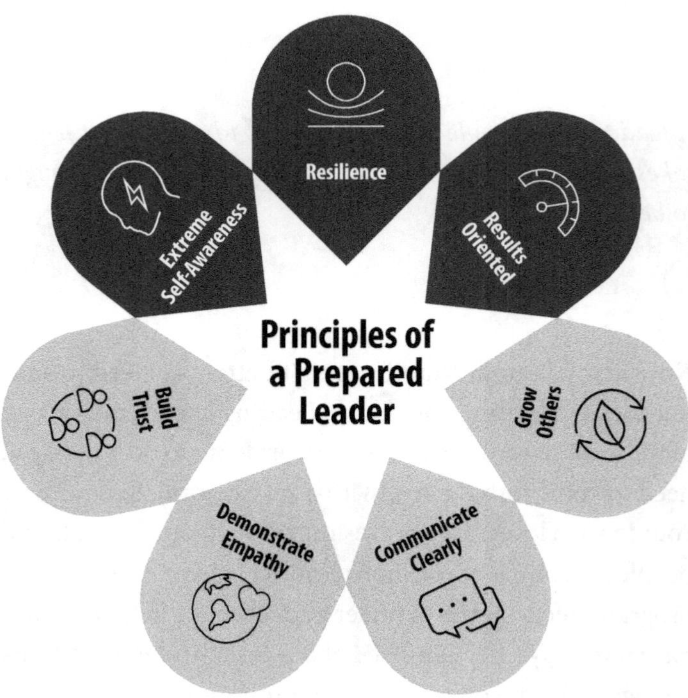

Each of these chapters includes exercises and reflection questions that will help you apply what you're learning. In many cases, I provide planning documents that can be reused over and over again. It will be important to stop reading and complete the activities as you go through the chapters or make a list of activities you want to come back and revisit.

The real magic of this section is in the tools, so don't skip over them. Try them out and let me know what you think! I love hearing your success stories. You can also find printable worksheets of many of the activities and planning documents on my website. Just go to *www.RashleighConsulting.com/Book* to grab a copy.

With all that said, let's get to work!

CHAPTER 7

BUILDS TRUST

"Building trust is a process. Trust results from consistent and predictable interaction over time."

—BARBARA M. WHITE.

Think of a leader you've worked for that you trusted. Go ahead. I'll wait.

Got one? Great! Now think about what specific things they did to make it easy for you to trust them. Were they hard working? Could you tell they were caring? Did they have integrity? Were they self-aware?

Now, think about a leader you've worked for that you didn't trust. Why didn't you trust them? Did they take credit for your work? Were they unavailable? Did they play favorites? Did their mood change dramatically from day to day? Could you tell they weren't being transparent? Chances are good that it was a combination of these qualities or behaviors that pushed you over the edge. Maybe you trusted them for a while, then there was a straw-that-broke-the-camel's-back moment where you had enough and there was no going back.

Real question....do you think they got up in the morning and thought, "You know, today I'm going to go to work and really make sure that these people don't trust me. In fact, I'm hoping they totally hate me and think of me as the worst leader they've ever had?" I just don't think they did. I think 99 percent of leaders wouldn't intentionally do something to a member of their team that would affect their trust and would be horrified to hear that they had. Trust breakdowns happen in the minute-to-minute interactions we have with people, big and small, and they have long lasting consequences.

Trust is a physical force. You can feel it when it's present and when it's not. It's like the air we breathe. We can take it for granted but we sure notice it when it's gone. Trusting others comes easier to some than others. Our ability to trust can be influenced heavily by our personalities and life experiences. If people have given you many reasons to not trust, then it might be harder for you to extend trust to others. Our ability to forgive others is also a factor. Those who find it easier to forgive can usually push through trust breakers more quickly than those that may struggle to forgive or tend to hold a grudge.

Don't be fooled into thinking trust is just a squishy people-related topic that doesn't impact results. It impacts them at a massive level. In fact, research shows "that the cost of too little trust is even higher than the cost of too much. Economists comparing the economic growth of various countries have found a strong positive correlation between GDP growth and measuring social trust. One study found that a 10 percent increase in trust translated to about a half percent increase in per capita income growth and even a positive effect on employment rates." (Buttigieg, 2020)

In my opinion, the military is the best model for building trust with others quickly. I've had the privilege of working alongside the military while I was a CIA employee. Leadership matters in military culture because lives are on the line. Bad leadership decisions can lead to lives lost. There's no choice but to get it right. Their culture of trust and integrity is transparent and is critical to long-term mission success. It has long been studied as an example of what to do as leaders and trust is at the heart of it.

The United States Army's own post-World War II research revealed that "those military units that had high trust and confidence in their unit leaders showed a low rate of combat fatigue or shell shock. Conversely, those units whose soldiers reported that they neither trusted nor liked their leaders showed an extremely high rate of combat fatigue or shell shock, sometimes as much as ten times more than the units who trusted their leaders." (Klann, 2003)

> What was the difference maker between the units with high-trust leaders and low-trust leaders? The high-trust leaders clearly communicated that they cared about their soldiers and that they were committed to keeping them safe. They also treated the soldiers with respect and were authentic in their communication. They kept their word and were effective communicators. (Klann, 2003)

Author Simon Sinek has noticed that high-trust military organizations "have cultures in which the leaders provide cover from above and the people on the ground look out for each other. This is the reason they are willing to push hard and take the kinds of risks they do." All this can and should be applied outside of military organizations, especially during times of crisis.

So how do you build and keep trust with others? One of my favorite models for thinking about building trust is from Stephen M.R. Covey's book *Speed of Trust*. In it, he describes trust building as making deposits in a piggy bank. If the bank is nice and full because you've spent time building the relationship, it is more likely to survive if you have a trust breakdown. The stronger the back account is, the stronger the relationship is at its core.

Deposits could include things like being transparent, taking ownership when things go wrong or even saying thank you. Often, it's the little things that help us build trust with others. Being consistent in our behavior and acknowledging and knowing the people around us go a long way to building relational trust at work.

Building trust is especially important for service-based leaders. "Trust is a prerequisite for servant leaders, because the leaders must trust that the employees are worth serving and that they, and the organization, will benefit from their service. Practicing servant leadership generates trust in the employees, who may be inspired by their manager's competence and character and convinced by their manager's serve-first practice that he or she has their best interests at heart. Trust is one of the means to achieve servant leadership, and it is also an end that is achieved by servant leadership," Covey says. (Tarallo, 2018)

We tend to trust ourselves because we know what our intention is, but other people judge us based on our behavior, not by our intention. Once when I joined a team, the leader asked me to stop by his office every morning to say hi before I went to my office. I of course followed the request, but it also ticked me off. I thought it was a way for him to see what time I was coming in each day and as a new mom, I really resented that kind of oversight. It made the beginning of my day even more stressful than it already felt.

Then one morning, I forgot and about fifteen minutes after I sat down at my desk, he came looking for me. The first thing out of his mouth was, "Oh good you're okay! I was worried. You're always at work by now." He was legitimately concerned about my safety. That's when I remembered that he was a former major in the army. He had worked in areas where safety wasn't a guarantee and he took his responsibility to keep us safe seriously. I never forgot to check in with him again.

This story is a great example of how important it is to share what the intention is behind our requests. That's why one of my biggest pieces of trust building advice is to just start stating your intention more often. That can sound like:

- "My intention in having this conversation with you is to help you become the leader I know you have the potential to be."

- "My intention for having this staff meeting is to bring us together to collaborate about some of the issues we've been having with our customers lately."
- "I'm asking you to work on this project because I know it will cause you to stretch and grow in new ways and you are ready for that challenge!"

So what do you do when things go wrong because they will? My advice is always to make sure you know what went wrong, acknowledge it, apologize and then intentionally make some trust deposits. This can sound like: "Thanks for bringing this to my attention. My intention was not to make you question your ability to trust me. I would never want you to feel that way and I'm truly sorry. Here's what I commit to doing moving forward to build your trust in me again." Are these conversations hard? You bet. Is it worth it? Always.

Reflection Activity: When do you need to be more transparent in stating your intentions? What words do you want to share with others? How can you build intention stating as a regular habit? Who might you need to repair trust with moving forward? What ideas do you have about how to start to build trust again?

CRISIS APPLICATION

When crisis occurs and the stakes are high, trust becomes even more critical. If you want people to work hard and take risks during crisis it has to start with trust. When I first started working in leadership development for the government, I was part of a small team. In fact, when I first joined my deployed group there were just two of us that officially worked as facilitators. I remember meeting my co-worker, who I'll call Linda, and immediately struggling to trust her. She came across as a know-it-all and didn't seem to want to collaborate with or acknowledge the work of others. I made a few tepid attempts at building a relationship with her during my first few months on the job, but I honestly made the decision to keep my distance.

Then I found out that we were being asked to recreate and facilitate a well-loved four-day learning experience. In order to start to prep for the content, I took the course. As I was sitting in the classroom soaking up the chemistry between the two current facilitators, I got really worried, really fast. They were fantastic and the trust between them could be both seen and felt. I knew to give our learners the best experience we could, we had some relationship work to do and it needed to start as soon as possible.

One evening at the end of class, I stopped by her office and asked if she had some time to talk. I shared my concerns and asked what we could do to start building a relationship worthy of the work I knew we were both committed to. We talked for easily an hour and a half. We talked about what the last few months of working together were like for both of us and what we could do to help each other. She also shared with me some history about her last assignment that was really affecting her ability to trust others. I learned that what I was seeing as "know-it-all" behavior was really her trying to prove to others that she knew what she was doing because she hadn't been respected in her last role. With that context, I could see her in a whole new light.

We left that office committed to having each other's back and continuing to share how we were feeling when things went wrong. Building trust with Linda was a slow, day-to-day process and it was worth it. In the three years we worked together, she became one of my closest friends. We built a relationship in the classroom that was a kind of synergy that's rare. We supported each other and had each other's back, always. As a new leadership facilitator, I also learned a ton from working with Linda. It was like going to facilitation college every day we worked together. I became a better learner and teacher because of her. None of that would have been possible without both tough conversations and a willingness to put a spotlight on trust. All this work prevented what could have been a detrimental crisis for our team from occurring. If we hadn't come together as a facilitator team, thousands of students would have been affected.

Simon Sinek says, "Being a leader requires having people that choose to follow you. Trust must be established before anyone will make the decision to follow you. Trust doesn't emerge simply because a customer makes a decision to buy something. Trust is not a checklist. Fulfilling all your responsibilities does not create trust. Trust is a feeling that begins to emerge when we have a sense that another person or organization is driven by things other than their own self-gain."

When things get tough, pay close attention to trust. How do you build it? How is trust between the members of your team? How much do you trust your leaders? The answers to these questions will guide you and help you lead your team out of crisis.

BUILDS TRUST RECAP

- Trust is a physical force. You can feel it when it's present and when it's not. It's like the air we breathe. It can't be faked.
- High trust leads to big results, including better financial results.
- You can think of trust as making deposits and withdraws in a bank account or piggy bank. The more deposits take place the more likely the relationship is to survive when withdraws happen.
- If you want to build trust with others, start using the phrase "my intention is/was" more often.

DEMONSTRATES EMPATHY

"Leadership is about empathy. It's about having the ability to relate and connect with people for the purpose of inspiring and empowering their lives."

—OPRAH WINFREY

Now more than ever, there is a consistent failure in the modern workforce to cope with emotions. That failure to cope is contributing to increased burnout rates, higher stress levels, and depression rates that are four to five times the normal average. (Amen, 2020)

Research from MIT Sloan suggests that "emotions are running high. The disruptive events characterizing 2020—a global pandemic, climate-related disasters, economic uncertainty, and social discontent—are leading employees to bring a higher level of emotionality to work than ever before." Many of us have been trained to try and keep our emotions under cover while in the workplace, and that is only causing more harm. That same research shows that "there are long-term costs to keeping emotions buried and that, if stifled, they will erupt in counterproductive ways. By supporting emotional expression within their teams, leaders can help their organizations function at their best." (Sanchez-Burks, 2021)

One of the most proven ways to support that emotional expression is through empathy, regardless of world events. Brené Brown defines empathy as "connecting with people so we know we're not alone when we are in struggle." Businessolver, an employee benefits consulting company, conducts one of the most extensive workplace empathy studies and has for five years. They found that "year over year, empathy continues to play a key role for employees considering where they would take employment, their salary, their work effort, and whether they will stay at their current organization." Their research also shows that for many leaders, this could be a huge blind spot as "91 percent of CEOs say their own company is empathetic, but only 68 percent of employees agree."

The Center for Creative Leadership analyzed data from 6,731 managers in thirty-eight countries searching for more trends on empathy. They found that "empathy in the workplace is positively related to job performance. Managers who practice empathetic leadership toward direct reports are viewed as better performers in their job by their bosses."

When you are leading a team of people in times of crisis, there is no behavior you'll need to lean into more than empathy. Unfortunately, no one teaches us how to demonstrate empathy in business school. Creating a culture of support during tough times is essential and too often isn't done. This isn't because people don't understand the need, but out of a lack of ability to demonstrate empathy well.

Empathy expert Liesel Mindrebo Mertes works with organizations to help train them on how to use empathy in the workplace. While talking about her business mission Liesel shared, "What I'm trying to encourage people and organizations to do is to practice more meaningful check-ins with each other. When you practice empathy regularly, it actually allows you to deal with those disruptive life events much earlier and be much more helpful instead of always cleaning up the mess after things go wrong."

Before I had the privilege to get to know her personally, I heard her speak at an event a few years ago. Out of an evening full of ten to fifteen speakers, I remembered her message most clearly because her work is personal to her. Liesel has experienced big losses in her life, and she speaks with experience about what truly helps when you are facing tough situations.

She shared this with me: "When you are supporting others through tough situations, you can do so through meaningful words and meaningful gestures. Organizations often don't apply these concepts consistently. Their implementation of meaningful gestures is based on what kind of leader and team they are on. So, a highly emphatic team sets up meals for two months, but another team does nothing. I encourage organizations to think about what the standard things are we can do for everyone."

WHAT TO DO

Empathy expert Liesel Mindrebo Mertes recommends that leaders and colleagues also avoid saying things like, "Tell me what I can do to help." She explained, "That phrase ends up being unhelpful because what it's really asking that person—who is already, emotionally, physically, spiritually at their limit—is to extend themselves creatively in the moment, to know exactly what they might need. Most people can't do that in the moment, and it can be difficult to ask someone to go grocery shopping for you."

Instead, she said, "Make a specific offer that you can commit to and feel comfortable doing. Something like, 'I'd love to send you a DoorDash gift certificate. What's your email address?' or 'I'm making a Costco run today. What are some things I can bring you?'"

Often, it's the small gestures during hard times that take minutes to perform that people remember and cherish. I've had the privilege of working for two leaders in my life who were exceptional at this and they both demonstrated it through handwritten notes.

The first was a human resource leader I worked for named Laura. She was an amazing leader for hundreds of reasons, but the thing I remember about working for her almost twenty years later is the notes she would write to us every payday. Back in the day when you used to actually get a paycheck in an envelope, she would walk down to the payroll department and pick up our checks for us. Then she would take them into her office and spend ten to fifteen minutes writing notes on the outside of the envelopes. Our jobs were often hard, and stress levels always seemed to be high. The note was always personal and also tied to the work we had completed the last few weeks. It was a small but meaningful gesture of her appreciation for our hard work, and it was an immediate mood lifter. Our team started calling them "Laura's Love Notes," and if she wasn't in the office on payday, we would all take our checks and leave the envelope on her desk because we wanted our note!

The second was a leader during my time working for the government. The head of the department that I worked in sent a handwritten note to our house any time something big happened in our lives. I received notes from him every time I was promoted or received a performance award as an acknowledgment of that work. But I also received notes from him when my grandma died and when my son was born. Many of those notes came while I was not working for him but deployed to an entirely different organization. That small gesture always amazed me because I knew he did it for all five hundred to one thousand employees that worked in that department. He was also gifted at remembering those events. The next time I would see him in the hall, he would always comment on the latest thing that happened to me. It mattered to me that he saw me as not just an employee, but as a person.

Reflection Activity: What comes most naturally to you during tough times? Are you an excellent cook and love providing meals to others? Do you love dogs and would happily dog sit or dog walk for someone? Are you happy to give money for group gifts or meals? Spend some time reflecting on what your signature gesture

can be when you need to support others. If you focus on just one that most people will find helpful, it makes it easier to make the offer of support when the need arises.

WHAT TO SAY

When it comes to meaningful words, too many of us lean into cliches like, "They are in a better place" or "You were lucky to have the person with you for so many years." Because knowing what to say to support people is hard, we tend to resort to things people have said to us. Sadly, those things aren't always good. Though it may be uncomfortable, there is a truth you need to understand. As Liesel has told me before, "Some things can't be fixed. They can only be carried. If someone's marriage is falling apart, there's nothing you are going to say that is suddenly going to not make that painful."

So, what do you say? I recommend in these types of situations that you lean into asking questions, listening, and validating what the person shares with you. Let's put this in a scenario. Let's say that a coworker's father was just placed in hospice care. You might say something like: "I just heard about your father. I'm so sorry that this is happening. How are you and your family doing?"

Then listen. Really listen.

Too often, we don't engage with people who are experiencing crisis because we don't want to bother them or don't know what to say. A good friend of mine lost her first child, Parker, three days after his birth. I still remember having no idea what to say or how to support her during that time. As she's lived with that loss for the past thirteen years, I often remember something that she said to me a few years after Parker died. She told me, "No one lets me talk about him. It's too hard for them, and they don't know what to say, but really I just want the space to remember him." People often do want to talk about what they are experiencing. Provide that space if you are able.

You can also lean into a coaching skill called validation. Validation is basically just acknowledging that an emotion is happening and normalizing it. That can look like: "You seem really upset about this and that is so normal. Anyone in your shoes would feel that way."

You can pair that validation with a helpful question like, "What can I do for you that would feel like help right now?" or a gesture like, "I was thinking of you this morning and grabbed a gift card for your favorite restaurant. I just wanted to take thinking about feeding the kids tonight off your plate."

Also know that you are going to get it wrong sometimes. Apologize if you need to, learn from it, and do better next time. The scenario that I shared about a colleagues' father being placed in hospice was real, and I didn't do a good job displaying empathy when it happened.

I lost my grandmother about nine years ago, and it ended in a very tough hospice stay. She was in a coma for two to three weeks while we held vigil waiting for her to die. It was horrible, and I have memories from that time that I frankly wish I didn't. The experience was traumatic for my family.

My coworker's situation triggered that trauma for me, and it's hard to display empathy with others when you are triggered.

When I found out about his father dying, instead of leaning in, learning more, and offering help, I told him what happened to my grandmother. In graphic detail. It's one of the biggest empathy-misses I've ever had in my life. Instead of focusing on him, I made it about me. A few hours after our conversation, I went back to him and apologized, and because he's a good human he forgave me. But I've learned from that experience and try to do better, and that is all we can expect from ourselves and each other.

Every single day you have opportunities to demonstrate empathy to your team members and colleagues. Do it well, and it can be the difference maker for the success of both you and your employees.

DEMONSTRATING EMPATHY RECAP

Some phrases to say:

- Tell me more about what's happening for you right now.
- You seem really sad, and that's so perfectly normal right now.
- I'm so sorry that you are going through this, and I'm here to help in whatever way I can.
- I'm bringing dinner by at 5:30. What do you like on your pizza?

Some things to avoid:

- Sharing the time it happened to you.
- Cliches like "they're in a better place."
- Trying to sugarcoat things.
- What can I do?

Prepare in advance by:

- Knowing your team. What are their favorites? What does care look like to them?
- Spending time with your team members.
- Encouraging a spirit of caring among your team.
- Know what your signature meaningful gesture is and be prepared to provide it.
- Apologize when you get it wrong.

CHAPTER 9

COMMUNICATES CLEARLY

"The difference between mere management and leadership is communication."

—WINSTON CHURCHILL

Imagine it's a typical morning and you're starting your day with a bowl of your favorite cereal. As you begin eating, you notice something strange in the bowl. You study it and it appears to be a shrimp tail. Just how freaked out would you be? That's what happened to Jensen Kemp one morning as he was eating a bowl of Cinnamon Toast Crunch. He took his outrage to Twitter and tweeted a picture of two shrimp tails with cinnamon sugar on them and tagged the maker of the cereal, General Mills.

What followed was a lesson in how not to handle a potential publicity issue. Instead of acknowledging the potential issue, General Mills issued this tweet in response: "After further investigation with our team that closely examined the image, it appears to be an accumulation of the cinnamon sugar that sometimes can occur when ingredients aren't thoroughly blended. We assure you that there's no possibility of cross contamination with shrimp." (Valinsky, 2021) Unfortunately, the situation continued to get out of hand with Kemp continuing to tweet about the exchange expressing his concern about the company's response and their lack of customer service and General Mills continuing to double down on its assurances that it could not possibly be shrimp tails.

Sadly, there is also no resolution to the story because Kemp stopped tweeting about the story after getting some unrelated bad press. Regardless, the story got national attention and certainly could affect the company's credibility long term.

The lesson? What we say and do, especially when things go wrong, matters. The best practice is to acknowledge the problem, apologize, and then take action to resolve the complaint. Admitting mistakes and communicating well is a sign of humility and high self-awareness and should be modeled by leaders.

I think few leaders would argue that communication isn't an essential function of leadership. Research from SpriggHR tells us that "an effective leader needs to be a skilled communicator, applying that skill in relationships at the organizational level, in larger communities and groups, and sometimes even on a global scale. However, according to the statistics, 57 percent of employees report not being given clear directions, and as much as 69 percent of managers are not comfortable communicating with their employees in general." That looks like the very definition of a growth opportunity to me.

But how do you actually become a better communicator? It starts with putting some time and energy into your communication. With a bit of reflection and planning, you can become a drastically better communicator. There are three areas that I like to focus on: communication channels, adapting to your audience, and transparency.

COMMUNICATION CHANNELS

Unfortunately, I see too many leaders who either don't prioritize communication or seem to be reactive in their communication strategy. Leaders have a tremendous ability to impact the communication practices and norms of their team. I often recommend that leaders take a good look at how information gets communicated on their team. This looks like identifying the practices that are currently in place and evaluating whether they are working.

A few years ago, I had a client that came to me completely overwhelmed by the number of emails she was receiving every day. We took a look at where the emails were coming from and the trend was that 50 to 60 percent of her emails were coming from her direct reports. I asked, "Is that the best way for your team to communicate with you?" Her response was, "No. I'd much rather they come to me directly or save questions for our next meeting." Unfortunately, she'd never told her team about that preference. They were assuming that email was the best way to get a response because she was responding. To shift that took a bit of reflection and a team effort to think about how and when information is communicated.

Communication channels and practices also need to be adapted and evaluated when crisis occurs. Karly Cope, VP of Talent at Community Health Network, was part of daily, network-wide command calls during the height of the COVID-19 surge. Part of her evaluation and restructuring of communication channels during this crisis involved adding regular communication points with her team. In order to ensure that her team also received critical information she shared with me that "right afterward, I would either have a live call with the whole department or an email. Honestly, I was worried about the impact it was having on the team. I was communicating intense information like 'here's how many ventilators are left.' I started asking the team about how the information is affecting your day. I got overwhelming feedback from the team to not stop the calls. They appreciated the consistency of knowing that we would all talk once a day, every day. It helped alleviated anxiety. It didn't even matter what we were talking about."

In my conversations with leaders, this appeared to be a trend. When I spoke with Market Operations Manager at PNC Bank Lindsey Hicks, she said that "impeccable communication is critical during times of crisis. You need to be succinct, but clear. Also, I really took a look at the cadence of when I was meeting with my staff and mirrored what our branches do. We now have a morning and evening touch base to set the tone for the day and the debrief. We think about how things went, what did we learn and what do we need to follow up on."

For both of these organizations, daily huddles were not a typical communication channel, but the pandemic required an adaptation.

COMMUNICATION CHANNEL

ACTIVITY: COMMUNICATION CHANNELS REFLECTION

Use the chart below. Think about how you and your team are using the communication channels available to you. Is it working? What ideas do you have for how it could be used differently? Revisit this chart periodically, especially in times of crisis. When the stakes are high or the workload intense, you may need to adapt your communication methods.

	HOW IT'S USED	HOW'S IT WORKING	IDEAS FOR CHANGE
Email			
Texting			
Phone Calls			
1:1 Meetings			
Team Meetings			
Video Calls			
Instant Messaging			

ADAPTING TO YOUR AUDIENCE

Great leaders, especially great service-oriented leaders, adapt their communication style to their audience, whether that audience is an employee, a customer, or the boss. There are many ways to think about adapting to your audience, but I like to think of two specific things: method and length. The method can be summed up easily by just understanding what communication methods your audience prefers the most. The best way to find that information out is to simply ask. I like to have a conversation with my direct reports and my boss where we dig into methods based on the situation or type of information. How do they like to receive praise? In person? One-on-one? In a team meeting? What's the best way for me to reach them in a true emergency? How much do they value team meetings and what type of information do they like me to share? By opening up the dialogue you can learn someone's preferences and then try your best to honor them.

Length of communication can often be evaluated based on what you know about someone's personality. Do they tend to communicate in action items and bullets? Do they like to give a lot of detail? Do they ask follow-up questions? It's especially important to know these preferences when it comes to delegation conversations. Delegation is a skill many leaders I work with struggle with and it's a skill I've struggled with myself.

In my last leadership role, I worked with a team member who was incredibly talented. She had the perfect skill combination of technical know-how and creativity, and I relied on her heavily for the creation of program materials. However, the first couple of times we chatted about a project, I noticed that she seemed to want more details from me than I was providing. I love to give people creative freedom and as long as the big picture of the effort is honored, I tend not to care about the details. She really did care and also wanted to get a project right the first time. It took me a couple of months to learn that if I could show her some examples or even just reiterate that I trusted her to come up with something amazing, it made it easier for her to deliver results. That little switch was easy for me to make and made sure that we were both getting our needs met. That's what adapting your communication style can look like in action.

DELEGATION PLANNER

Delegation Planner Activity: The next time you need to delegate a new task, use the planner below to think through the conversation.

WHAT'S THE TASK?

EXPECTED COMPLETION DATE:

WHAT'S THE IMPACT OF THE TASK? WHAT WILL BE IMPROVED?

WHAT ARE THE POTENTIAL CHALLENGES?

WHAT SUPPORT IS NEEDED?

WHEN WILL FOLLOW UPS OCCUR?

COMMUNICATION PREFERENCES RESOURCE

Communication Preferences Resource: Use this to have
a conversation with your team members about their
communication preferences.

HOW DO YOU LIKE TO RECEIVE PRAISE?

WHAT'S THE BEST WAY FOR ME TO REACH YOU IN A TRUE EMERGENCY?

HOW MUCH DO YOU VALUE TEAM MEETINGS? WHAT'S IMPORTANT FOR
YOU DURING A TEAM MEETING?

WHAT TYPE OF INFORMATION DO YOU LIKE ME TO SHARE WITH YOU?

DO YOU PREFER DETAILS OR THE BIG PICTURE?

NOTES:

TRANSPARENCY

When the pandemic hit, President of ADVISA Heather Haas took a hard look at communication and made some key decisions. She told me, "I knew transparency would be critical so for maybe six months, I sent out video updates. Every week, I would share what was important at that moment, the three things we all needed to focus on in the week ahead. I felt it was important to create a clear line of sight directly to me and to the rapidly shifting priorities of the organization. We also got incredibly transparent about the financial side of the business—here's where we are and here are our concerns and current thinking on how we will handle them. I know people were worried and I wanted to pull back the curtain and reduce anxiety with honesty."

Transparency builds trust and it's not as hard as we sometimes think it is. An article from BlogIn says that "the context of transparency in an organization's actions and the team's communication is as simple as it is: No secrets. It is taking actions in such a way that others can easily see them. People like to know things. No one feels comfortable being surrounded by secrets and hidden information, especially in the workplace."

The bottom line: share what you are able, as soon as you can. It helps people trust you and the organization.

SPECIAL CONSIDERATIONS FOR LEADING REMOTELY

I mentioned in the first section of this book that the recent research on working remotely presents several challenges for leaders to work to address. One study shows that "over one-third of office workers say this email fatigue is likely to push them to quit their jobs. One in three (33 percent) of employees say an excess of video calls is the most unpleasant part of remote work. Over two in five (44 percent) of remote workers dream of the day without video calls and one in four (25 percent) crave a notification-free day." (Brown, 2021) That's a large chunk of workers who are struggling to keep up with remote work and all that comes with it. So, how do we help our teams cope with this new way of working? The communication method reflection could be a real help in this area. Take a hard look at how and when your team is communicating. Is it all necessary? What can be reduced?

Research has shown that there are a few things that you need to keep a close eye on when team members work remotely. Because collaboration can go down, things like brainstorming new projects to start can suffer. Organizational culture can also be greatly impacted and is especially challenging to instill in new hires. Additionally, because mentoring and coaching so often happen in the moment, working remotely requires leaders to set time aside for feedback and coaching intentionally. (Kane, 2021)

Reflection Activity: *How much of your team is currently working remotely? Approximately how much time are you spending with them each week? Is that amount enough? When was the last time you provided feedback and coaching?*

But it's not all bad news. One really great shift that's happened as a result of remote work is that it's leveled some of the power dynamics of meetings. When you meet via Zoom there's no head of the table or back row. Everyone is shown on the screen as an equal.

When I worked at the CIA there's a common practice called "back benching." Rank and seniority matter. To sit at the main meeting table, you have to have proven yourself. Around each meeting room's walls are chairs and that's where you sit until you've earned a literal spot at the table. If something you've been working on needs to be reported at the meeting, your boss or a more senior member of the team presents the information from the table and you sit along the wall in case a question gets asked that needs details you can provide.

That culture is there for a reason but makes it very difficult for newer, lower ranking members of the team to be heard. Zoom meetings take those types of power dynamics out of play and I think that's an incredibly bright side to working remotely. I'd also challenge you to think about how this could be maintained if and when work returns to in-person.

Another positive is that research is showing that "organizations and individuals have had no choice but to discover new ways of working. Many have reported successfully implementing years' worth of digital transformation plans over the course of a few months. For example, mortgage loan company Freddie Mac implemented remote building inspection, and many health care providers pivoted rapidly to telemedicine. Even companies that needed to maintain a significant co-located workplace used digital innovations to improve employee and customer engagement and safety. For example, Hitachi adapted sensors to monitor social distancing in factories, and many restaurants quickly adopted virtual ordering and delivery services." (Kane, 2021)

Crisis creates a need to shift, and if leaders can take advantage of the innovation that comes from crisis once the crisis has passed, they could be even more successful.

COMMUNICATING CLEARLY RECAP

- What we say and how we say it matters.
- Be sure you understand the communication channels that you are using, why you are using them, and if they are effective. You get to decide how and when you communicate with your team.
- Great leaders, especially great service-oriented leaders, adapt their communication style to their audience, whether that audience is an employee, a customer, or the boss.
- Transparency builds trust and it's not as hard as we sometimes think it is.
- Remote work has led to new challenges and opportunities.

CHAPTER 10

GROW OTHERS

—

*"The higher you climb, the more your success depends on mak-
ing other people successful. Leaders are judged by what their
followers achieve. Leadership is elevating individuals to do
more than they thought possible and groups to do more than
their members could do independently."*

—ADAM GRANT

In my eight years at the CIA, the organization was led by five different directors. My favorite of those leaders was General Michael Hayden. He came into an organization that was struggling to rebuild credibility and processes post-9/11 and was also struggling with morale. He said, "My goal when I got to the CIA wasn't to shake things up. It was to calm things down." (General Michael Hayden on Leadership, 2013)

That's exactly what he did. General Hayden quickly built trust with employees at all levels. At least once a week he ate lunch in the cafeteria and took pride in just sitting down with a random table of employees and getting to know them. Employees, including myself, loved seeing him out and about.

As a leadership development professional, I also loved having a true leader at the helm of the organization. It was easy to use him as a case study for what great leaders do. He often told organizational leaders that "the first job of a leader is to create more leaders." He expected all CIA leaders to continue to grow and develop themselves and their teams. It was a true privilege to get to watch him lead.

The job of a leader is to get results through other people. To do that well you need to have a commitment to growing others. When I ask leaders what they enjoy most about being a leader, easily 75 percent respond that they love helping their teams grow and develop. That's true for Emily McGinnis, a leader at Taysha Gene Therapies. She told me, "The coaching part of my job is my favorite part. I love helping younger members on my team. If I can help other people grow and meet their objectives, that means a ton to me at the end of the day."

That development-focused mindset is even more important if you are leading millennials. In a research study by Gallup, "59 percent of millennials say opportunities to learn and grow are extremely important to them when applying for a job. Comparatively, 44 percent of Gen Xers and 41 percent of baby boomers say the same. Millennials assign the most importance to this job attribute, representing the greatest difference between what this generation values in a new job and what other generations value." (Adkins, 2016)

Unfortunately, many leaders don't provide meaningful development opportunities. Gallup suggests that "Managers need to know how each employee best learns and ensure that he or she is learning through various outlets. These outlets could include new responsibilities and tasks that allow employees to expand their knowledge and experience such as planning an event, managing a project or leading a meeting. But employees should also have an opportunity to take part in more formalized learning through classes or coursework." (Adkins, 2016)

Forming a strong relationship, providing regular feedback, and discussing potential future roles or career development isn't difficult. It just takes prioritization. Too many leaders just don't take the time to focus on employee development, or they fail to lean into one of their greatest assets as a leader: coaching.

LACK OF TIME

So how do you prioritize growing others? Build development into the processes you already have in place, like onboarding. Think through what will help new team members get up to speed and acclimated as quickly as possible. Be sure to set aside time on your calendar to spend time with new team members. Don't let yourself get so overbooked that you have no time to make new team members feel comfortable. In my last corporate role, I would set at least thirty minutes aside to meet with new employees every day during their first few weeks. That ensured we had time to go through critical information and cover any questions they might have. I would then taper that time off to thirty minutes three days a week, then two, then one.

Setting aside intentional time with new hires also gives your new hires time to get to know you and provide feedback about what they still need to learn. Michael Timmes, a leadership expert, consultant and coach with the national human resources provider Insperity says, "During onboarding, after the initial introductions, getting-acquainted conversations, and explanations about how operations work, the servant leader should solicit the new hire's observations, impressions and opinions. This conveys the message, from the onset, that the employee's thoughts are valued. If a manager is not spending at least 25 percent of his or her time developing future leaders, then you're really not fulfilling your responsibilities as a leader." (Tarallo, 2017)

Over time, you can slowly give new hires more and more freedom and spend less time hands on. Timmes says, "Another way to enhance the talent development process is to selectively relinquish power, so that employees can lead certain projects and take ownership of initiatives. Giving up power, and having others lead—that builds confidence in people." (Tarallo, 2017)

Once an employee is functioning well in their role, continue to check in regularly. Ask a development related question every time you meet one-on-one with a team member. Here are some great questions to ask:

- What development opportunities would help you be more successful in your current role or work towards a promotion?
- What's your biggest struggle at work right now?
- What would you like to learn more about right now?

- Do you have the resources you need to do your job?
- What reading have you done lately to stay up to date in your field?

The goal here is to just open a dialogue. When you talk about growth and development regularly your employees will know that you think it's important, and they will be that much more likely to come to you to chat about what type of development opportunities they want to explore.

COACHING SKILLS

One of the best development tools at a leader's disposal is their ability to provide on the job coaching. Coaching at its core is really just helping someone discover what actions they might take and then providing accountability and support around those actions. It's not a hard skill to learn but it can require a shift from a problem-solving mindset to a more curious mindset. Leaders love to help people solve problems. To be an effective coach you just need to shift from a telling approach to an asking approach.

To start leaning into this skill, the next time an employee comes to you with an issue or problem, ask some questions. I love to use what I call a "Fast Coaching Method." Start by asking the employee to tell you more about what's happening. Then ask them what they've done so far to try and solve the problem. From there, ask them what's something they could do to solve the issue. Finally, wrap up the conversation by asking them what support they need from you to take action.

This approach is fast and incredibly effective. By guiding the employee through key questions, they will come up with their own potential solution, and we are all much more likely to follow through with actions that were our idea. Continue to use this approach and over time your employees will develop exceptional problem-solving skills.

FAST COACHING METHOD
1. Tell me more.
2. What have you tried so far?
3. What's one thing you could do?
4. How can I support you with that action?

Activity: Use the "Fast-Coaching" reference card to have a coaching conversation with one of your employees. You can find it at www.RashleighConsulting/Book/Resources.

This method can also be incredibly effective when employees are struggling. However, you need to understand where to focus your coaching attention. Often as leaders, we tend to coach or correct based on behavior or action. But our thoughts drive how we feel about the situation and ultimately the actions we take. If you're struggling to get an employee to change their behavior, ask them what they think about the situation and coach those thoughts. This coaching could sound like this:

You: "I've noticed that the last few project reports you've submitted aren't complete. That's not like you. Can you tell me more about what's happening?

Employee: "Well I've been struggling to get my work done lately. There just seems to be too much to do and honestly, this report doesn't seem as important as the other work on my plate."

You: "I know we've had a lot of new work on our plate lately and that's been tough. Tell me what you know about how this report is used."

Employee: "I don't know. I've never seen it used at all."

You: "I bet that's frustrating. Let me pull back the curtain a bit on the report for you. I send these project reports along to the company CEO so that she is able to quickly see our progress each week. I know she reads and values these updates and the work you are doing."

Employee: "Oh, I didn't know they were read by the CEO. I'll make sure they are complete in the future."

This may sound like an extreme example, but just as Simon Sinek's work tells us, employees often don't understand why they are doing the work they are doing. If we can find out the thoughts that are driving their actions, we can get to behavior change much more quickly. This is also a great method to change your own behavior. If you're struggling to shift your behavior in an area or situation, reflect on your thoughts and feelings. They are often the key to behavior shifts.

 ***Reflection Activity**: Try out the Thought/Feeling/ Action approach on yourself using this worksheet. Think about a situation you currently face that you*

wish you could change. In the first column, write your current thoughts and feelings. What actions are you taking? How are they serving or not serving you? Now, what thought could you choose that might shift that outcome? What would that help you feel and do? What might the likely outcome be?

THOUGHT/FEELINGREFLECTION

Thought

New Thought

Feeling

New Feeling

Action

New Action

Outcome

New Outcome

CRISIS APPLICATION

I love the musical *Hamilton*. I get knocked out by the pure creativity of someone reading a one-thousand-page book about Alexander Hamilton and becoming inspired to write a rap and hip-hop-filled musical about it. But I also love the way *Hamilton* highlights the mentor/mentee relationship between George Washington and Alexander Hamilton. It's a lesson in how to develop and grow others. That relationship starts during the American Revolution, certainly a time of crisis for the entire country. Washington is constantly trying to help Hamilton avoid the mistakes he made in his life and career. At every turn, he develops and molds Hamilton and helps him channel his sharp intellect into constructive paths. Washington reminds him that "History has his eye on you." Much of Hamilton's legacy can be attributed to the leadership and mentoring that Washington provided him.

This example drives home the point that employee development doesn't become less important during times of crisis. If anything, it becomes more important. However, development can be one of the first things to be put on the back burner. Don't let that happen! Get creative if needed. Check in via text or in shorter time blocks but continue to regularly check in on your employees.

Crisis also often provides opportunities for employees to step up. As your plate gets more overloaded, look for appropriate delegation opportunities. Let your employees help in different ways. New projects and tasks can be a development opportunity in itself. Education and training budgets often get dramatically scaled back or cut altogether during times of crisis. Providing development opportunities on the job is a great way to offset the potential impact of those cuts.

One employer that took this approach was tech retailer Verizon. When the company had to close down some of its retail locations, it allowed many of those employees to apply transferable skills to other areas of the business. Verizon gave employees a choice of career paths and then implemented personalized learning, with the goal of enabling these workers to close any skill gaps before moving on to new roles. Verizon's approach is a best practice for how to take care of employees when big re-organizations occur because they didn't lose sight of the people affected by the change. (Del Rowe, 2020)

Crisis can be a great development tool. By continuing to prioritize development and utilizing on the job coaching and development, your employees can come out of crisis stronger and more prepared for what comes next.

GROW OTHERS RECAP

- The job of a leader is to get results through other people. To do that well you need to have a commitment to growing others.
- Too many leaders just don't take the time to focus on employee development or they fail to lean into one of their greatest assets as a leader: coaching.
- Ask a development related question every time you meet one on one with a team member.
- Use the fast-coaching approach to guide employees through tough situations.

- Thoughts drive our feelings and our feelings drive our actions. If you want to foster behavior change in yourself or an employee, uncover the core thought.

CHAPTER 11

BURNOUT REVISITED

———

"Almost everything will work again if you unplug it for a few minutes...including you."

—ANNE LAMOTT

Early in this book, I showed you some dramatic data about burnout rates. To remind you, in 2019, estimates of job burnout have been reported as high as 44 percent among employees at some point in time, according to Gallup. (Wigert, 2020) We can only assume that number is now higher. The causes vary but research from Healthline shows that "being exposed to continual stress can cause us to burnout. Feelings of exhaustion, anxiety, and isolating from friends and family members can be some of the signs."

Burned-out employees are less productive, less creative, and more likely to leave an organization. So, what can you do to help? Start by honing your skills in noticing the symptoms of burnout, then look for specific ways you can help.

HOW TO RECOGNIZE BURNOUT

Research from Culture Amp shows that burnout affects employees at every level. They may experience physical symptoms like headaches, fatigue, appetite loss, and shortness of breath. Are any of your employees taking more days off than usual? Do they seem tired or lethargic? Mental symptoms can include spending more time worrying or having trouble focusing. Sleep can also be dramatically affected by burnout. Do the people on your team seem more tired or distracted? Is anyone complaining about work/life balance? On an emotional level, people can have a shorter than usual fuse or struggle with their coworkers. You may also notice more cynicism or that the employee is starting to distance themselves from their work. If someone who is usually pretty levelheaded suddenly starts a fight in every meeting, that could be burnout.

Overall, watch for changes. Listen for things like:

- "I don't feel my usual connection to my work."
- "I need a vacation."
- "I just can't seem to get caught up."

Brand new research that was highlighted in the book *Burnout: The Secret to Unlocking the Stress Cycle,* also shows that burnout symptoms can also occur due to a lack of emotional processing skills. This research shows that "emotions are tunnels. If you go all the way through them, you get to the light at the end. Exhaustion happens when we get stuck in an emotion." We can get stuck due to chronic stress, a fear of breaking social norms, or because it just seems safer than feeling the emotion. (Nagoski, 2019)

In order to come out the other side of the emotional tunnel, we have to complete the stress cycle. Research has found that there are several ways to do that including physical activity, deep breathing, positive social interaction, laughter, affection, crying, and creative expression. (Nagoski, 2019)

When you notice these symptoms, have a conversation with the employee. Ask what you can do to help and acknowledge that they seem to be suffering from burnout symptoms. Employees who experience burnout are less effective and more likely to leave. The earlier you can intervene and try to assist, the more likely you are to help the employee and get things turned around. You can also check in during regularly scheduled meetings. Saying something like "Tell me about last week" can give you pretty clean insight into how things are going. Be sure to try and uncover the root cause of the burnout. That will help you address the right problem. Remember it could be a non-traditional cause like lack of connection to the company of the work they are doing.

When I spoke with Heather Haas, ADVISA president, she said, "I try to be very aware of myself when I am reaching burnout and I try to be very aware of my team. If I'm seeing something, I can say, 'You seem really stressed out. Let's talk about that. How can I help?' and I try to open as many of those doors as I can. You have got to be really savvy to pick up on depression and burnout in people who don't want you to pick up on their depression and burnout, especially when they can continue to perform at a high level through it."

Heather's approach is a best practice and a great reminder that our top performers can often mask the symptoms of burnout well. It's important to connect with each employee and engage with them on their level of burnout.

BURNOUT REFLECTION

Activity: Use this grid to capture any symptoms of burnout you've noticed in your employees.

Employee Name		
	OBSERVED	**NOTES**
Overload		
Exhaustion		
Distracted		
Less engaged		
Missed work		
Other		

STRATEGIES TO REDUCE BURNOUT

When employees are suffering from burnout, one of the best places to start is to encourage them to take some time off. Clear any obstacles that might be standing in the way. Reassign work if needed and be sure that either you or someone else on the team is handling any emergencies that come up. Let the employee truly disconnect from work. Time off with interruptions won't do the trick. They need to be able to fully check out.

After some time off, encourage burned out employees to set some boundaries around work. Encourage them to turn off email notifications on their phone or take a lunch break with a friend. Help them brainstorm ways they can get a bit of a break during the day or other things that would help them feel more connected to work. As I mentioned in the "Resilience" chapter, sleep is also critical to bouncing back from burnout symptoms.

Vice President of Talent for Community Health Network Karly Cope confirms this approach. She said, "You've got to know your team and what works best for them. It might be cleaning their house or turning off phone notifications. Whatever it is, help them find the time for it."

Karly is a former leader of mine and I remember when I started working on her team, she encouraged me to do something I'd never done before. She asked me not to install email on my phone. Based on our conversations she knew I was coming out of a rough job and that I was burnt out. She encouraged me to take the pause that I needed to recharge, learn a new organization, and tap into the creativity I needed to do what she needed me to do in my role. I'll always be grateful for that pause.

She naturally did what many leaders don't. She validated that burnout shouldn't be the norm. Employees shouldn't think that the bar for success is working themselves into the ground. If your organizational culture encourages overwork, take a hard look at what you might be doing to reinforce that culture. If we want happy, healthy, engaged employees, we can't expect them to kill themselves for their jobs.

RETAINING WOMEN IN THE WORKFORCE

I can't write a book about leading in times of crisis and fail to address the elephant in the room. When big, global crises happen to the world and organizations, they affect women differently than men. Research shows that during the pandemic "more than one in four women are contemplating what many would have considered unthinkable just six months ago: downshifting their careers or leaving the workforce completely." (Coury, 2020) The COVID-19 pandemic and the shutdowns that came with it drove women from the workplace at an alarming rate, mostly due to the lack of childcare that came with school and daycare shutdowns. According to the Rand Corporation more than 2.2 million women have left the workforce since the beginning of the pandemic. (Swift, 2021)

It's hard to fully understand the long-term impact of this mass exodus but what is clear is that it will affect the future of work for years to come. There are certainly systematic changes like paid maternity leave, discounted day care, and more flexible work environments that could help shift this dynamic for women, but don't underestimate the impact you can have as a leader. It may take some creativity, but you can make it easier for women to thrive at work.

When my son, Sam, was born in 2009, I worked on a team with phenomenal leaders. I remember when I told my boss I was pregnant; the first thing out of his mouth was "Work can be whatever you need it to be when you come back from leave. Just let me know how much you want to work." I knew working full time in a high-paced, high-stress role and caring for my son was going to be a huge challenge. I also knew that I was likely only going to have one child and I didn't want to miss his newborn days. I asked to take five months off for maternity leave and then to come back two, ten-hour days per week to start. My amazing boss said no problem.

However, my experience was not typical. Most women don't have the flexibility to do important, professional work part-time and I was incredibly grateful for the flexibility. But my situation also highlights a disparity that often happens. I was able to take the time I wanted to take to be with my son, but I was also expected to make career sacrifices as a woman.

As Sam hit the toddler stage and I got more comfortable with the idea of spending more time at work, I slowly upped my hours and added two mornings to the mix. One of those mornings Sam spent at a pre-school and for the other, my husband stayed home with him until I got home, then worked later into the evening. I remember telling my co-workers about the arrangement and everyone just going on and on about what a great dad my husband was and how lucky I was to have his support. Their reaction was shared by everyone who knew about the arrangement and the more I heard it the madder I got. For over a year, I was home with my son three days a week and was still able to contribute financially to our household. Do you know how many people praised me and told me what a great mom I was? Zero.

When women take time off work to care for children it's expected, but when men do, it's applauded. This double standard seeps into the culture of organizations and sends a message to women that they have to do more. According to a United Nations report, "The modern woman still does nearly three times as much unpaid domestic work as a man." (Rodsky, 2019) And that work is rarely acknowledged. That's both wrong and counterproductive.

So what can you do to support and retain women at work? First, be willing to have candid conversations about work/life balance and flexibility for all your employees, not just the women. Make it clear that your organization supports flexibility and understands that for many people family comes first. It can't just be lip service. It needs to be part of your culture.

Second, proactively provide leadership development opportunities. When I was still a junior officer at the CIA, I attended a round table event with a well-respected female senior leader. Many of the women in the room asked questions about work/life balance because the leader had two teenage children. I'll never forget her words. She said, "You can't have it all. Anyone who tells you that is lying. I made the choice to have a career and when I have to make hard choices my children often come second."

The message was that you can't be a good leader and a good mother. I believed that message for easily five years. I now know that's completely false. There are so many women who do both well. Culturally, we have to step away from these types of messages and keep encouraging women to step into leadership roles. Burnout can look different for women and it's important to address it differently when needed. Our organizations will be better because of it!

According to research from the Stanford School of Business, burnout also costs corporations between $125 and $190 billion per year in additional healthcare spending. (Smith, 2019) In order to have healthy organizational bottom lines, we have to address burnout for our employees and make changes that get everyone working at their best.

BURNOUT REVISITED RECAP

- As many as half of your employees could be suffering from burnout.
- Burnout can sound like:
    - "I don't feel my usual connection to my work."
    - "I need a vacation."
    - "I just can't seem to get caught up."
- To help reduce burnout symptoms:
    - Encourage time off.
    - Help employees set boundaries around their work.
    - Encourage more sleep!
    - Ask questions to get to the root cause of the burnout then do what you can to help.
- To retain women in the workforce you may need to address their burnout symptoms differently.

CONCLUSION

—BILL OWENS

Many people think that the strongest, toughest, most cut-throat leaders are those who would thrive in a crisis environment, but the opposite is true. As we've seen through stories and hard data, highly empathetic, focused, and values-driven leaders are better able to keep their teams engaged and thriving.

The more prepared we are as leaders ahead of any crisis, the better our odds for success and survival. In order to thrive, you need to know who you are before a crisis hits. Crisis leadership is when opportunity meets preparation. That's why applying the Principles of Prepared Leadership is so important. Crisis doesn't define us. It's the work that we do before challenges and obstacles happen that makes leaders shine.

In addition to crises unique to your specific working environment, several workplace crises exist for leaders to navigate.

Burnout affects at least 44 percent of workers right now, and that number is likely much higher. Mental illnesses like depression, anxiety, and languishing are at all-time highs. Remote work is likely here to stay, and many leaders are struggling to lead their teams remotely. But remember, a workplace crisis that needs to be managed by leaders will typically contain three additional elements.

1. A threat to the organization.
2. The element of surprise.
3. A short decision time. (Management Study HQ, 2021)

That can happen anytime, sometimes as often as daily.

Now that you know the Principles of Prepared Leadership, you can use them to become the leader your team needs you to be. In fact, now that you know the Principles of Prepared Leadership, you must use them. Your team is depending on you!

Crisis-proof leaders demonstrate extreme self-awareness. They know who they are, why they do what they do, and what they value. They consistently seek out learning opportunities and dive into personal development even when it's uncomfortable. If a leader doesn't pursue extreme self-awareness, that leader is likely to overestimate their own skills and gloss over very real problems their team members point out. Not pursuing self-awareness produces leadership that enables problems rather than solves them.

Crisis-proof leaders are resilient. They work against any blind spots to practice resilience in their everyday life through the six factors of vision, composure, collaboration, reasoning, tenacity, and health. Leaders that don't focus on their personal resilience, especially when leading in times of crisis, will burn out.

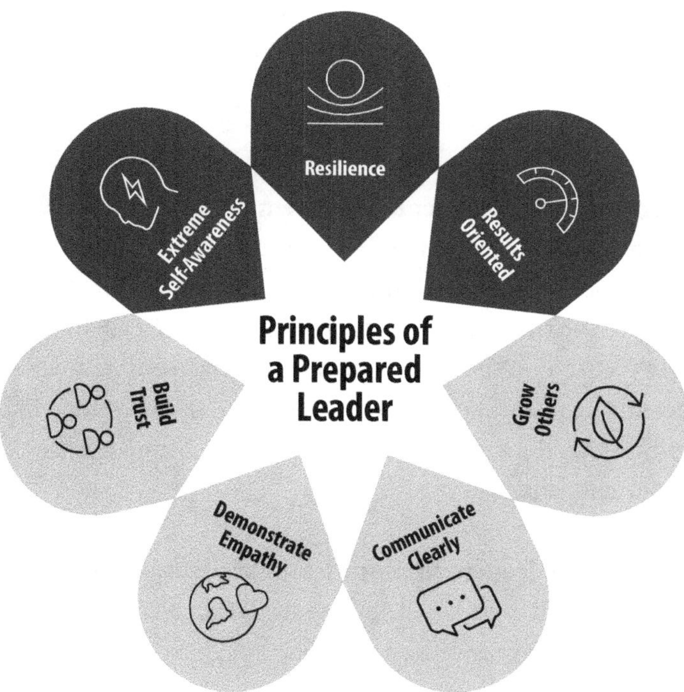

Crisis-proof leaders are results-oriented. They use a combination of social skills and concentration on results to motivate and inspire others. They are willing to have clear and kind feedback conversations to help their team improve and they have channels in place for employees to share potential problems so they can be solved before they become a crisis. Leaders who don't will face crisis after crisis as problems remain unresolved and employees become increasingly disengaged.

Crisis-proof leaders build trust. They know that high trust leads to big results, including better financial results. They declare their intentions and motives to others and repair trust when needed. They know that without trust, nothing else is possible.

Crisis-proof leaders demonstrate empathy. They know how to support their team members through meaningful words and actions. They don't hide from hard times but instead work to support those who may be experiencing them. They stay focused on their employees and their needs as a whole person. Leaders who don't will find that employees don't like to be treated as if they are cogs in a machine and they'll experience turnover.

Crisis-proof leaders communicate clearly. They know that what they say and how they say it matters. They are clear about the communication channels they use, why they use them, and evaluate their effectiveness. Great leaders, especially great service-oriented leaders, adapt their communication style to their audience, whether that audience is an employee, a customer, or the boss.

Crisis-proof leaders grow others. They understand that the job of a leader is to get results through other people. To do that well you need to have a commitment to growing others. Unlike so many leaders, they take time to focus on employee development and they regularly lean into one of their greatest assets as a leader: coaching.

When I started my own business, I leaned into a motto I've had for years: No More Bad Bosses! I hope you'll consider making that a personal charge for yourself as well. Bad leaders have an impact on their team. They will consistently produce unhappy workers. When people are unhappy at work, they take that unhappiness home, and often their most important relationships struggle. But by leaning into some behavioral tweaks, you can ensure that you don't become one of those bad bosses. All it takes is focus and the willingness to keep getting better.

I'm often asked what the CIA and healthcare, the only two fields I've ever worked in, have in common. It's crisis. I love to work with leaders who are leading teams with big missions, big goals, and high stakes. The goal isn't just to grow the bottom line. Lives are at stake and those high stakes usually bring plenty of crisis situations along with them. And what I've seen in the way of effective versus ineffective leaders in these situations has led me to where I am now, teaching a myriad of leaders how to better prepare for the crises that will inevitably come.

I'm grateful to have written this book. I wrote this book to be a guide as you work to become the leader the world needs you to be, both day to day and in crisis. My hope is that as you've read it, you feel like you have someone in your corner helping you along the way but now it's time to act.

Start with yourself. What can you give to others? Where do you need to lean in and do more learning to be as effective as possible? What do you wish your leader did for you? Then act and experiment. Try some of the techniques and tools in this book.

Everything we've covered is something you can do. None of it is out of your reach. Good leaders make the world a better place. Now go be one of them and know that I'm here cheering for you every step along the way!

ACKNOWLEDGMENTS

Writing this book has truly taken a village of early supporters, cheerleaders, friends, and family who loved me through and in spite of this creative process.

This book was made better by the leaders and experts who shared their time and their stories with me so freely. I am so grateful for the contributions of Monica Cepero, Heather Haas, Darryl Lansey, Jason Barnaby, Liesel Mertes, Karly Cope, Lindsey Hicks, Shannon Kunberger, Mark Ferrara, Stephanie King, Julie Stufft, and Emily McGinnis.

I spent only two short years working at Community Health Network but the leaders I worked with and had the privilege to teach have truly become family. A big thank you goes out to each of you for your support and love! That list includes Larissa Davids, Sharon Johnson, Allyson Hurst, Jason Houston, Carrie Wilson, Travis Lozier, Sherri Noble, Thomas West, Karen Snyder, Angie Trussel, Sarah Rankin, Kelly Coffey, Cynthia A. Spann, Karen Katz, Karrah Poole, Autumn Yohler, Michelle Harrold, Chloe Moushey, Diane Reynolds, Angie Rush, Chris Summers, Jacquelyn Whobrey,

Mike Moreman, Deshini Moonesinghe, Jennifer Hindman, Nino Voskuhl, Shannon Kunberger, Stacy Fackler, Laura McMichael, Bente Weitekamp, Carol Shields, Adrianne Slash, Ashley Hatfield, and Amy Ambs.

Special shout out to my Trimedx clan who all these years later never fail to have my back including Jessica Blankenship, Tracey Draschil, Denisa Lambert, Kathy Martis, Debbie Johnson, Rhiannon Lawson, Michael Rusbasan, and Tammy Gordon.

Thanks to Bram Koerts, Ari Campbell, and Gayle Smith for your early support of this book!

Thank you to my peers and colleagues who have never once viewed me as competition and cheer loud and hard for every success I have including Angie Woods, Erin D Slater, Deseri Garcia, Tami Chapek, Hannah L Northup, Jenni Robbins, Maryann Lombardi and Terry McDougall.

Meeting monthly with the amazingly talented Beth St. Clair, Rachel Pritz, Liesel Mertes, Brandon Wilson and Jason Barnaby makes me a better human. Thanks to each of you for all you've done and continue to do for me daily.

I am incredibly grateful for the friendship of Julie Breckenfelder and the wise coaching of Karyn Taeyaerts. This book exists because of your support!

I'm so blessed to call some amazing women my sisters including Stacie Colston, Shelley Winterberg, Jennifer Court, Erin Weesner, Amy Strasburger, Kelly Canada, Amy Upp,

Elizabeth Grant, Lindsay Hicks, Daria Weingartner, Kenzie Isaacs, Kristin Kramer, and Kristi Timmons.

Some co-workers just become part of your family like Kathy Swasey, Darryl A. Lansey, Kimberley Condas and Kendra Lamirata. Thanks for continuing to make me better!

Sharon Tebbe, Amber Wilfley, Kamie Hubbs, Jerry Walker and Gretchen Hasler all came into my life in different ways, but each is an amazing part of my fan club. Thanks for being you!

I'm so grateful to have gotten a chance to teach with Cindy B. for a few years. You made me a better teacher, facilitator, coach and friend. We'll forever be Bindy!

Every now and again in life, you get to work for an amazing leader. Karly Cope, I'm so glad I got a chance to be a part of your team. Watching your example made me a better leader. Thanks for cheering first and loudest and for being as into the West Wing as I am! If I had a carving knife, I would give it to you.

A big thank you to the incomparable Nate Pfhaler. I'm so glad we just happened to live in the same dorm! I can't imagine my life without your friendship. I'm so glad you married Jennifer Pfahler who is equally as amazing!

Eric Koester made this journey possible. Thanks for sharing your knowledge, your heart and your infinite ideas. Cynthia Tucker walked me through the hard road of editing and revisions and I'm grateful for your help and guidance. Anne

Snyder was the best Developmental Editor a girl could ever hope to have. You were such a gift during a hard and rewarding process. Thanks for everything. I literally don't have the words and this book would contain zero words without you!

To my dad who showed me what it means to be a leader and my mom who gave me a teacher's heart: I'm so lucky to call you my parents. Thanks for loving me, always.

To Matt, my rock, my cheerleader, my love...thanks for always believing in me more than I believe in myself. I'm so glad you're mine.

And finally, to Sam, thanks for sharing your mom and for giving me so many reasons to have hope in the future. You make me so proud!

APPENDIX

————

INTRODUCTION

Mendoza, N.F., "COVID-19 has exacerbated a 75% job burnout rate, study says." *Tech Republic*, August 24, 2020. *https://www.techrepublic.com/article/covid-19-has-exacerbated-a-75-job-burnout-rate-study-says/*

World Health Organization. *"Guidelines for the Primary Prevention of Mental, Neurological and Psychosocial Disorders."* Geneva. *https://apps.who.int/iris/bitstream/handle/10665/60992/WHO_MNH_MND_94.21.pdf*

CHAPTER 1: CRISIS AND LEADERSHIP

Johnson and Johnson Corporate. "Our Credo." Accessed September 23, 2021. *https://www.jnj.com/credo/*

Knight, Jerry. "Tylenol's Maker Shows How to Respond to Crisis." *Washington Post*. October 11, 1982. *https://www.washingtonpost.com/archive/business/1982/10/11/tylenols-maker-shows-how-to-respond-to-crisis/bc8df898-3fcf-443f-bc2f-e6fbd639a5a3/*

Management Study HQ. "What is Crisis?" Accessed March 15, 2021. *https://www.managementstudyhq.com/what-is-crisis-and-different-types-of-crisis.html*

Oxford Languages Online. "Crisis." Accessed August 23, 2021.

The Keep It Simple Stupid in Crisis Guide: Understanding the effects of stress in crisis decision making. Noggin Website White Paper.

CHAPTER 2: WHY NOW?

Amen Clinics (blog). "1 in 3 Americans are Suffering from Anxiety and Depression—Are You One of Them?" Posted June 2, 2020. *https://www.amenclinics.com/blog/1-in-3-americans-are-suffering-from-anxiety-and-depression-are-you-one-of-them/*

Brown, Eileen. "Remote Workers Now Say Email Fatigue and Notifications are Worse Than Commuting." *ZDNet*, April 22, 2021. *https://www.zdnet.com/article/remote-workers-now-say-email-fatigue-and-notifications-are-worse-than-commuting/*

Fruga, Juli. "How to Identify and Prevent Burnout." *Healthline. https://www.healthline.com/health/tips-for-identifying-and-preventing-burnout#takeaway*

George, Bill. "The Pros and Cons of Working Remotely." *Fortune*, April 17, 2021. *https://fortune.com/2021/04/17/remote-work-home-hybrid-model-future/*

Grant, Adam. "There's a Name for the Blah You're Feeling: It's Called Languishing." *New York Times*. April 19, 2021. *https://www.nytimes.com/2021/04/19/well/mind/covid-mental-health-languishing.html*

Kruse, Kevin. "How to Lead with Empathy, Remotely." *Forbes*, April 7, 2021. *https://www.forbes.com/sites/kevinkruse/2021/04/07/how-to-lead-with-empathy-remotely/?sh=408629502fac*

Vasel, Kathryn. "To Prevent Burnout, LinkedIn is Giving Its Entire Company the Week Off." *CNN Business*, April 5, 2021. *https://www.cnn.com/2021/04/02/success/linkedin-paid-week-off/index.html*

Wigert, Ben. "Employee Burnout: The Biggest Myth." *Gallup* (Blog). March 13, 2020. *https://www.gallup.com/workplace/288539/employee-burnout-biggest-myth.aspx*

World Health Organization. "Burn-out an Occupational Phenomenon: International Classification of Diseases." Posted May 28, 2019. *https://www.who.int/news/item/28-05-2019-burn-out-an-occupational-phenomenon-international-classification-of-diseases*

World Health Organization. "*Guidelines for the Primary Prevention of Mental, Neurological and Psychosocial Disorders.*" Geneva. *https://apps.who.int/iris/bitstream/handle/10665/60992/WHO_MNH_MND_94.21.pdf*

CHAPTER 3: WHAT IS LEADERSHIP?

Greenleaf. "What is Servant Leadership?" Accessed February 28, 2021. *https://www.greenleaf.org/what-is-servant-leadership/*

Johnson, Sandhya. "Servant-Leader Heroes at Southwest Airlines." LinkedIn, December 1, 2017. *https://www.linkedin.com/pulse/servant-leader-experts-southwest-airlines-sandhya-johnson/*

Merriam-Webster Online. "Leadership." Accessed February 26, 2021.

Morella-Olson,Melinda. "12 Lessons in Employee Experience Strategy = Improvement in Customer Experience." *Imaginasim* (Blog). Accessed April 17, 2021. *https://www.imaginasium.com/blog/employee-experience-strategy#:~:text=Put%20 employees%20first.&text=Southwest's%20philosophy%20is%20 happy%20employees,customer%20and%20for%20the%20company.&text=This%20means%20trusting%20employees%20 will,great%20care%20of%20their%20customers.*

Oxford Languages Online. "Leadership." Accessed February 26, 2021.

Sandberg, Sheryl. *Lean in: Women, work, and the will to lead.* London: W H Allen, 2015.

Sinek, Simon. *Leaders Eat Last: Why Some Teams Pull Together and Others Don't.* New York: Penguin Group, 2014.

Tarallo, Mark. "The Art of Servant Leadership." *Security Management,* March 2017. *https://www.asisonline. org/security-management-magazine/articles/2017/03/ the-art-of-servant-leadership/?_t_id=8yEa3b8FuoYiS-DOGiKOD8A%3d%3d&_t_uuid=vBUdGvH1RBSNd_ov32Ct-vA&_t_q=servant+leadership&_t_tags=language%3aen%2csit eid%3ab1140b07-9e31-4808-809a-878911c7f3f1%2candquery-match&_t_hit.id=ASIS_Models_Pages_SMArticleDetail-Page/_6af1ea0f-ffc8-4753-9475-db52a0d23044_en&_t_hit.pos=1*

Wolfsteller, Pilar. "Southwest Posts Full-Year Loss for the First Time Since 1972." *Flight Global,* January 28, 2021. *https:// www.flightglobal.com/strategy/southwest-posts-full-year-loss-for-the-first-time-since-1972/142183.article#:~:text=That%20 47%2Dyear%20streak%20is,the%20same%20period%20of%20 2019.*

CHAPTER 4: EXTREME SELF-AWARENESS

Brown, Brené. *Dare to Lead*. London: Vermillion, 2018.

Lencioni, Patrick. *The motive: Why so many leaders abdicate their most important responsibilities*. Nashville: John Wiley & Sons, 2020.

Popova, Marie. "Fixed vs. Growth: The Two Basic Mindsets That Shape Our Lives." *Brain Pickings* (blog). January 29, 2014. *https://www.brainpickings.org/2014/01/29/carol-dweck-mindset/*

PR Newswire. "The Benefits of Self-Awareness in Difficult Times." *Market Insider*, March 22, 2020. *https://markets.businessinsider. com/news/stocks/know-thyself-new-study-looks-at-the-benefits- of-self-awareness-in-difficult-times-1029020025*

Salerno,Ryan. "34% of Americans Aspire to Have Leader- ship Positions," *Smart Recruiters* (blog), November 4, 2014, accessed February 23, 2021. *https://www.smartrecruiters.com/ blog/34-of-americans-aspire-to-leadership-positions/*

Sinek, Simon. *Start with why: How great leaders inspire everyone to take action*. Harlow: Penguin Books, 2011.

CHAPTER 5: RESILIENCE

Ellin, Abby. "Special Report: Why Developing Resilience May Be the Most Important Thing You Can Do for Your Well-Be- ing Right Now." *Everyday Health*, December 17, 2020. *https:// www.everydayhealth.com/wellness/state-of-resilience/#:~:- text=The%20majority%20of%20Americans%20overestimat- ed,Why%20is%20this%20important%3F*

Overby, Stephanie. "Emotional Intelligence: How to Stay Calm in High-Pressure Situations." *Enterprisers Project*, August 20, 2019. *https://enterprisersproject.com/article/2019/8/emotion- al-intelligence-how-stay-calm-under-pressure?page=0%2C0*

Rossouw, J.G., Rossouw, P.J., Paynter, C., Ward, A., Khnana, P. "Predictive 6 Factor Resilience Scale—Domains of Resilience and Their Role as Enablers of Job Satisfaction. *International Journal of Neuropsychotherapy*, 2(1),(October, 2017) 25-40.

Sanders, Laura. "How Coronavirus Stress May Scramble Our Brains." *Science News*, May 24, 2020. *https://www.sciencenews.org/article/coronavirus-covid19-stress-brain*

Wilcox, Gloria. "Feeling Wheel", January 1, 1982. *https://commons.wikimedia.org/wiki/File:The_Feeling_Wheel.png*

CHAPTER 6: RESULTS-ORIENTED

Brown, Brené. *Dare to Lead*. London, England: Vermillion, 2018.

Carroll, Lewis. *Alice's Adventures in Wonderland*. New York: Macmillan, 1920.

Covey, Sean, Jim Hurling, and Chris McChesney. *Four Disciplines of Execution*. London, England: Simon & Schuster, 2015.

Klann, Gene. *Crisis Leadership: Using Military Lessons, Organizational Experiences, and the Power of Influence to Lessen the Impact of Chaos on the People You Lead*. Greensboro, North Carolina: Center for Creative Leadership, 2003. *https://www.ccl.org/wp-content/uploads/2020/03/crisis-leadership-center-for-creative-leadership-guidebook.pdf*

Lieberman, Matthew. "Should Leaders Focus on Results, or on People?" *Harvard Business Review*, December 27, 2013. *https://hbr.org/2013/12/should-leaders-focus-on-results-or-on-people*

Scott, Kim. *Radical Candor: Be a Kick-Ass Boss Without Losing Your Humanity*. New York: St. Martin's Press, 2017.

CHAPTER 7: BUILDS TRUST

Buttigieg, Pete. *Trust: America's Best Chance.* New York, New York: Liveright, 2020.

Covey, Stephen M.R. *The Speed of Trust.* London, England: Simon & Schuster, 2008.

Klann, Gene. *Crisis Leadership: Using Military Lessons, Organizational Experiences, and the Power of Influence to Lessen the Impact of Chaos on the People You Lead.* Greensboro, North Carolina: Center for Creative Leadership, 2003. *https://www. ccl.org/wp-content/uploads/2020/03/crisis-leadership-center-for-creative-leadership-guidebook.pdf*

Sinek, Simon. *Leaders Eat Last: Why Some Teams Pull Together and Others Don't.* New York: Penguin Group, 2014.

Tarallo, Mark. "The Art of Servant Leadership." *SHRM* (Blog). May 17, 2018. *https://www.shrm.org/resourcesandtools/hr-topics/ organizational-and-employee-development/pages/the-art-of-servant-leadership.aspx*

CHAPTER 8: DEMONSTRATES EMPATHY

Amen Clinics (blog). "1 in 3 Americans are Suffering from Anxiety and Depression—Are You One of Them?" Posted June 2, 2020. *https://www.amenclinics.com/blog/1-in-3-americans-are-suffering-from-anxiety-and-depression-are-you-one-of-them/*

Brown, Brené. *Dare to Lead.* London: Vermillion, 2018.

Businessolver, *2020 State of Workplace Empathy Executive Summary.*

Sanchez-Burks, Jeffrey, Bradley, Christina, and Greer, Lindred. "How Leaders Can Optimize Teams' Emotional Landscapes."

MIT Sloan Management Review, January 4, 2021. *https://sloan-review.mit.edu/article/how-leaders-can-optimize-teams-emotional-landscapes.*

"The Importance of Empathy in the Workplace." *Center for Creative Leadership (Blog),* November 28, 2020. *https://www.ccl.org/articles/leading-effectively-articles/empathy-in-the-workplace-a-tool-for-effective-leadership/*

CHAPTER 9: COMMUNICATES CLEARLY

Brown, Eileen. "Remote Workers Now Say Email Fatigue and Notifications are Worse Than Commuting." *ZDNet,* April 22, 2021. *https://www.zdnet.com/article/remote-workers-now-say-email-fatigue-and-notifications-are-worse-than-commuting/*

Gerald C. Kane, Rich Nanda, Anh Phillips, and Jonathan Copulsky. "Redesigning the Post-Pandemic Workplace." *MIT Sloan Management Review,* February 10, 2021. *https://sloanreview.mit.edu/article/redesigning-the-post-pandemic-workplace/*

Katie Kavanagh, Nicole Voss, Liana Kreamer, and Steven G. Rogelberg. *"How to Combat Virtual Meeting Fatigue." MIT Sloan Management Review,* March 30, 2021. *https://sloanreview.mit.edu/article/how-to-combat-virtual-meeting-fatigue/?utm_source=newsletter&utm_medium=email&utm_content=more%20effective&utm_campaign=Enews%20BOTW%20 4/2/2021*

"The Importance of Leadership Communication in 2021". *SpriggHR* (Blog). September 1, 2020. *https://sprigghr.com/blog/leaders/the-importance-of-leadership-communication-in-2021/*

"Transparent Team Communication: Why and How to Embrace It". *BlogIn* (Blog). Accessed May 15, 2021. *https://blogin.co/blog/transparent-team-communication-why-and-how-to-embrace-it-69/*

Valinsky, Jordan. "The Cinnamon Toast Crunch Shrimp-Gate Didn't Have to Go Viral." *CNN Business*, March 24, 2021. *https://www.cnn.com/2021/03/24/business/cinnamon-toast-crunch-shrimp/index.html*

CHAPTER 10: GROW OTHERS

Adkins, Amy and Rigoni, Brandon. "Millennials Want Jobs to Be Development Opportunities." *Gallup* (Blog), June 30, 2016. *https://www.gallup.com/workplace/236438/millennials-jobs-development-opportunities.aspx*

Del Rowe, Sam. "Companies Prioritize Learning and Development in the Wake of Coronavirus Crisis." *EBN* (Blog). June 5, 2020. *https://www.benefitnews.com/news/companies-prioritizing-learning-and-development-in-the-wake-of-coronavirus-crisis*

Ogilvy Asia. "General Michael Hayden on Leadership." June 23, 2013. Video, 11:55. *https://www.youtube.com/watch?v=YoleoY-iBDRM*

Tarallo, Mark. "The Art of Servant Leadership." *Security Management*, March 2017. *https://www.asisonline.org/security-management-magazine/articles/2017/03/the-art-of-servant-leadership/?_t_id=8yEa3b8FuoYiS-DOGiKOD8A%3d%3d&_t_uuid=vBUdGvH1RBSNd_ov32Ct-vA&_t_q=servant+leadership&_t_tags=language%3aen%2csit eid%3ab1140b07-9e31-4808-809a-878911c7f3f1%2candquery-match&_t_hit.id=ASIS_Models_Pages_SMArticleDetail-Page/_6af1ea0f-ffc8-4753-9475-db52a0d23044_en&_t_hit.pos=1*

CHAPTER 11: BURNOUT REVISITED

Fruga, Juli. "How to Identify and Prevent Burnout." *Healthline.* *https://www.healthline.com/health/tips-for-identifying-and-preventing-burnout#takeaway*

Hamman, Chloe. "How to Recognize and Reverse Employee Burnout." *Culture Amp* (blog). *https://www.cultureamp.com/blog/how-to-recognize-and-reverse-employee-burnout#:~:text=Recognizing%20the%20signs%20of%20employee%20burnout&text=Physically%2C%20people%20may%20experience%20headaches,can%20be%20signs%20of%20burnout.*

Nagoski, Emily and Nagoski, Amelia. *Burnout: The Secret to Unlocking the Stress Cycle.* New York: Ballantine Books, 2019.

Rodsky, Eve. *Fair Play: The Hidden Costs of Doing It All.* New York: G.P. Putnam's Sons, 2019.

Sarah Coury, Jess Huang, Ankur Kumar, Sara Prince, Alexis Krivkovich, and Lareina Yee. "Women in the Workplace." Mckinsey & Company. September 30,2020. *https://www.mckinsey.com/featured-insights/diversity-and-inclusion/women-in-the-workplace*

Smith, Ryan. "Employee Burnout Costs Companies Big-Study." *Insurance Business Magazine,* July 31, 2019. *https://www.insurancebusinessmag.com/us/news/healthcare/employee-burnout-costs-companies-big--study-174125.aspx*

Swift, Jane. "Straddling The Fault Lines Of Work, Family And Sanity: How We Can Keep Women At Work." *WBUR* (Blog). February 17, 2021. *https://www.wbur.org/cognoscenti/2021/02/17/working-women-leaving-jobs-covid-child-care-economy-jane-swift?fbclid=IwAR0Sz-WLAUgcAU6uQ9H9n-WH4ffhXXHLN_en4Sq_4Nombbjh5rMMYvr29tA*

Wigert, Ben. "Employee Burnout: The Biggest Myth." *Gallup* (Blog). March 13, 2020. *https://www.gallup.com/workplace/288539/employee-burnout-biggest-myth.aspx*